• CELEBRATING HOLIDAYS & FESTIVALS AROUND THE WORLD •

Christmas & Hanukkah

Betsy Richardson

MASON CREST

Mason Crest
450 Parkway Drive, Suite D Broomall, PA 19008
www.masoncrest.com

Copyright © 2019 by Mason Crest, an imprint of National Highlights, Inc. All rights reserved. No part of this publication may be reproduced or transmitted in any form or by any means, electronic or mechanical, including photocopying, recording, taping, or any information storage and retrieval system, without permission in writing from the publisher.

Printed in the United States of America
First printing
9 8 7 6 5 4 3 2 1

Series ISBN: 978-1-4222-4143-1
Hardcover ISBN: 978-1-4222-4145-5

Library of Congress Cataloging-in-Publication Data is available on file.

Developed and Produced by Print Matters Productions, Inc. (www.printmattersinc.com)
Cover and Interior Design by Lori S Malkin Design LLC

QR CODES DISCLAIMER: You may gain access to certain third-party content ("Third-Party Sites") by scanning and using the QR Codes that appear in this publicat ion (the "QR Codes"). We do not operate or control in any respect any information, products or services on such Third-Party Sites linked to by us via the QR Codes included in this publication, and we assume no responsibility for any materials you may access using the QR Codes. Your use of the QR Codes may be subject to terms, limitations, or restrictions set forth in the applicable terms of use or otherwise established by the owners of the Third-Party Sites. Our linking to such Third-Party Sites via the QR Codes does not imply an endorsement or sponsorship of such Third-Party Sites, or the information, products or services offered on or through the Third-Party Sites, nor does it imply an endorsement or sponsorship of this publication by the owners of such Third-Party Sites.

• CELEBRATING HOLIDAYS & FESTIVALS AROUND THE WORLD •

Carnival

Christmas & Hanukkah

Easter, Passover & Festivals of Hope

Halloween & Remembrances of the Dead

Independence Days

Lent, Yom Kippur & Days of Repentance

Marking the Religious New Year

Ramadan

Ringing in the Western & Chinese New Year

Thanksgiving & Other Festivals of the Harvest

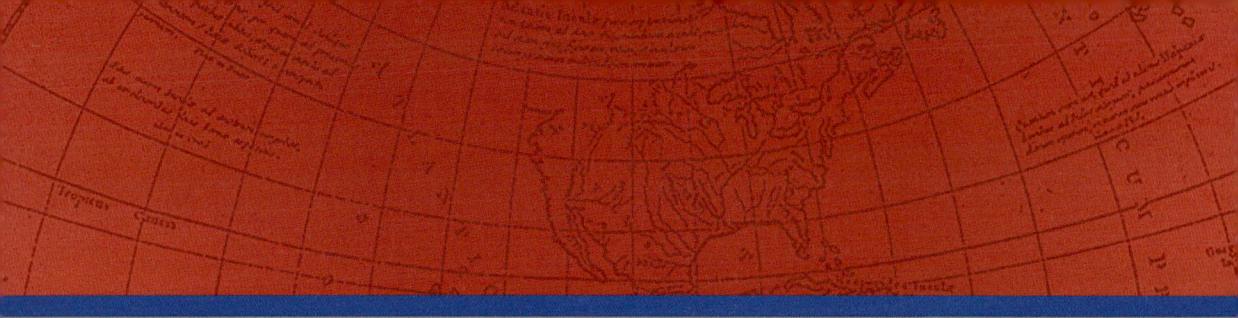

KEY ICONS TO LOOK FOR:

Words to understand: These words with their easy-to-understand definitions will increase the reader's understanding of the text while building vocabulary skills.

Sidebars: This boxed material within the main text allows readers to build knowledge, gain insights, explore possibilities, and broaden their perspectives by weaving together additional information to provide realistic and holistic perspectives.

Educational Videos: Readers can view videos by scanning our QR codes, providing them with additional educational content to supplement the text. Examples include news coverage, moments in history, speeches, iconic sports moments and much more!

Text-dependent Questions: These questions send the reader back to the text for more careful attention to the evidence presented there.

Research projects: Readers are pointed toward areas of further inquiry connected to each chapter. Suggestions are provided for projects that encourage deeper research and analysis.

Series glossary of key terms: This back-of-the book glossary contains terminology used throughout this series. Words found here increase the reader's ability to read and comprehend higher-level books and articles in this field.

CONTENTS

INTRODUCTION: Celebrating Holidays & Festivals Around the World **6**
INTRODUCTION: Christmas & Hanukkah **8**
1: Origins of Christmas **11**
2: Origins of Hanukkah **31**
3: European Traditions and Customs **49**
4: Latin American and Caribbean Traditions and Customs **69**
5: Middle Eastern Traditions and Customs **81**
6: North American Traditions and Customs **87**
SERIES GLOSSARY **106**
FURTHER RESOURCES **109**
INDEX **111**
PICTURE CREDITS **112**

INTRODUCTION

Celebrating Holidays & Festivals Around the World

Throughout human history, nations and peoples have marked their calendars with special days to celebrate, commemorate, and memorialize. Holidays mark time. They occupy a space outside of ordinary events and give shape and meaning to our everyday existence. They also remind us of the passage of time as we reflect on Christmases, Passovers, or Ramadans past. We set aside times to reflect on the past and future, to rest and renew physically and spiritually, and to simply have fun.

In English we call these extraordinary moments "holidays," a contraction of the term "holy day." Sometimes holidays are truly holy days–the Sabbath, Easter, or Eid al-Fitr, for example–but they can also be nonreligious occasions that serve political purposes, address the social needs of communities and individuals, or focus on regional customs and games.

This series explores the meanings and celebrations of holidays across religions and cultures around the world. It groups the holidays into volumes according to theme (such as *Lent, Yom Kippur & Days of Repentance*; *Thanksgiving & Other Festivals of the Harvest*; *Independence Days*; *Easter, Passover & Festivals of Hope*; *Ringing in the Western & Chinese New Year*; *Marking the Religious New Year*; *Carnival*; *Ramadan*; and *Halloween & Remembrances of the Dead*) or by their common human experience due to their closeness on the calendar (such as *Christmas & Hanukkah*). Each volume introduces readers to the origins, history, and common practices associated with the holidays before embarking on a worldwide tour that shows the regional variations and distinctive celebrations within specific countries. The reader will learn how these holidays started, what they mean to the people who celebrate them, and how different cultures celebrate them.

▲ In the Philippines, Christmas lanterns like these adorn churches as Catholics attend nine daily dawn masses before Christmas day. This centuries-old tradition was said to have been started by farmers who wanted to fulfill their religious obligation before their day's work in the field.

These volumes have an international focus, and thus readers will be able to learn about diversity both at home and throughout the world. We can learn a great deal about a people or nation by the holidays they celebrate. We can also learn from holidays how cultures and religions have interacted and mingled over time. We see in celebrations not just the past through tradition, but the principles and traits that people embrace and value today.

The Celebrating Holidays & Festivals Around the World series surveys this rich and varied festive terrain. Its 10 volumes show the distinct ways that people all over the world infuse ordinary life with meaning, purpose, or joy. The series cannot be all-inclusive or the last word on so vast a subject, but it offers a vital first step for those eager to learn more about the diverse, fascinating, and vibrant cultures of the world, through the festivities that give expression, order, and meaning to their lives.

INTRODUCTION

Christmas & Hanukkah

In the modern era, and particularly in the Western world, Christmas and Hanukkah have become major events in the calendar. The Christian festival of Christmas celebrates the birth of Jesus Christ, while Hanukkah celebrates a miracle that took place during biblical times. Although the events recalled in these holidays are unconnected, Christianity and Judaism spring from common traditions and holy books; in fact, their origins are so closely linked that people often refer to a Judeo-Christian tradition or heritage.

Both Hanukkah and Christmas take place close to the winter (or December) solstice–the shortest day of the year. Many ancient cultures celebrated this annual turning point. At a time when people are anxiously awaiting the return of longer days, both Christmas and Hanukkah are closely associated with light. For example, the central ritual of Hanukkah involves lighting candles every day for eight days. During Hanukkah, electric menorahs decorate public places where open flame is not permitted and are also sometimes placed in the windows of Jewish homes. Other symbols, such as the Star of David or the dreidel, frequently form part of light displays.

In the Christmas story, a star marks the stable where Jesus is born, and Christ himself was called "the light of the world." Most Christians would consider Christmas incomplete without lights decorating both their homes and the public spaces around them, not to mention special events such as candlelit church services.

Jews and Christians both consider sacred the 39 books that make up the holy scripture, or holy text. The Hebrew Bible or Tanakh, which is also known to Christians as the Old Testament, was composed before the birth of Jesus. Most of it was originally written in Hebrew, and it contains the history, prophecies, and knowledge of the ancient people of Israel. Judaism and Christianity both originated in the Middle East, and are Abrahamic—the term used to describe religions that honor Abraham, who was the leader of the tribes of Israel. For Jews, Abraham was the ancestor of all the Israelites.

▲ Christmas in warmer climates has a look all its own like these palm trees decorated with lights in Palma de Majorca, Spain.

Origins of Christmas

■ History of a Holy Day

Christmas is one of the most widely celebrated holidays in the world. Observed since the fourth century, today both Christians and many non-Christians celebrate the festival on December 24 (Christmas Eve) and 25 (Christmas Day). The word *Christmas* comes from a combination of the words *Christ's mass*. For Christians, Christmas is a time of joyful celebration as well as a time to express their faith, since the holiday commemorates the birth of Jesus. Most historians believe Jesus was a real person who grew up in Nazareth,

WORDS TO UNDERSTAND

Census: A count of the population.

Epiphany: January 6, which is observed as a church holiday. In Eastern churches, it is considered the date of Christ's birth. For others, it is observed in remembrance of the magis' visit to the baby Jesus.

Icon: A small religious painting, usually painted on wood; also a symbolic image such as an icon of a file folder on a computer screen.

Reenactment: The acting out of an event that took place in the past, such as historical events.

◀ The birth of Jesus, a symbol of joyful celebration, is at the heart of Christmas.

a town in northern Israel. However, the foundation of Christianity lies in the belief that Jesus was not just a person, but also the son of God—a divine being in human form. Among Christians, there are variations on this belief—some groups believe him to be one of three separate beings known as the Trinity (Father, Son, and Holy Spirit), whereas others believe him to be God in human shape.

The Hebrew Bible contains prophecies (predictions) about the future concerning a "Chosen One" (or *Messiah* in Hebrew) who will bring all the Jewish people to heaven. These prophecies also state that the Messiah will save all other people in the world by atoning for their sins and ridding the world of evil. Christians consider Jesus to be the Messiah, whereas most Jews believe that the Messiah is yet to come.

While the New Testament recounts the story of the Virgin Mary giving birth to Jesus in Bethlehem, it does not mention the actual date. Despite extensive research, historians still hold many conflicting opinions as to when Jesus was born. The early Christian church did not encourage celebration of the birthdays of people they considered saints or martyrs, including

▲ Pilgrims pray at the grotto, the site where Jesus Christ is traditionally believed to have been born, inside the Church of the Nativity in the West Bank town of Bethlehem.

Jesus. At the time, pagans, or people who believed in several gods, observed the birthdays of their religious figures. In an effort to distance themselves from pagan practices, the church preferred to recognize the day a person was martyred (killed) instead of his or her birthday. As a result, Jesus' birth was not treated as an important day on the religious calendar for nearly 200 years after the beginning of Christianity. Good Friday (which commemorates his crucifixion and death) and Easter (which celebrates his resurrection) were considered much more important. It was not until the ninth century that the church assigned Christmas its own liturgy, or religious service, known today as Christmas Mass. For many years, Jesus' birth was celebrated the same day as his baptism, on January 6. The Armenian Church as well as other Eastern Churches still celebrate Christmas on this date.

By the year 221, Jesus' birth was celebrated on December 25. This was due to the efforts of Sextus Julius Africanus, a Christian historian who wrote *A History of the World*. The first of its kind, *A History of the World* was an influential work that attempted to unite the account of the Bible with Greek and Roman history. In it Africanus introduced the idea that the world was created on March 21, and that on March 25, the fourth day of creation, God made light. He calculated that Jesus was conceived many thousands of years later on March 25. This is symbolically significant as Jesus is often referred to as "the light of the world." Additionally, nine months after March 25 is December 25, so the date became widely accepted as the date of Jesus' birth. However, not everyone agrees on this explanation as to why December 25 was the date chosen. Some suggest it was because it is near the time of the winter (December) solstice. Solstices are the days six months apart in the year when the difference in length between day and night is greatest.

Christmas shares orientation and timing with the celebration of the ancient Roman holiday of Saturnalia, which took place from December 17 to December 24, in honor of the God Saturn. Saturn was

THE STORY BEHIND "XMAS"

Some Christians are bothered by seeing Christmas written "Xmas," believing that the writer is too lazy to write Christ's name, or is trying to remove religious beliefs from Christmas. The abbreviation is actually at least 1,000 years old. It comes from the uppercase Greek letters X and P. The letters are an ancient abbreviation for Christ's name in Greek. In many Orthodox, Protestant, and Catholic churches the two letters appear with one laid over the other in an icon.

associated with agriculture and bountiful crops. As a remedy for the dark, dreary days of winter, the Romans focused on the coming spring. They lit candles and lanterns to push back the darkness, and celebrated with dancing, feasting, and merrymaking. For a brief time rich and poor were treated as equals, slaves might be served by their masters, people took part in masquerades, and a mock king—The Lord of Misrule—was crowned. Businesses, schools, and courts closed, and the citizens enjoyed life to the fullest.

Other pagan celebrations of the winter solstice continue to influence Christmas celebrations today. Since Celtic and Germanic tribes lived in the Northern Hemisphere, the solstice was very important—it signaled the return of longer days and the warmth of the sun. To mark the turning of the seasons, ancient Scandinavians and Celts cut gigantic logs and dragged them through the

▲ Greek Orthodox Christians take part in a Christmas procession. Eastern Orthodox Christians celebrate Christmas Day on January 7.

▲ The Serbian Orthodox bishop is shown here with his followers, who have gathered to watch the burning of the traditional Yule log of dried oak tree branches on Orthodox Christmas Eve, which is January 6.

forest to burn on their hearths. They called them "Yule logs." If the log burned for 12 days, it was thought to bring good luck. These tribes generally held trees to be sacred, symbolic of life itself, and inhabited by spirits. For the Scandinavians, any tree that stayed green, that is "evergreen," during their long and bitter winters must have magical properties. Mistletoe, which stays green throughout the year, was another plant the Celts considered sacred. The Celtic influence can be seen in the custom of hanging mistletoe, as well as in the evergreen and holly decorations often used at Christmas.

The people of ancient Rome also used holly in many of their celebrations. They even gave each other gifts of holly wreaths. Today holly has become a symbol of Christmas, and so has its colors: red and green.

▲ The people of ancient Rome used holly as a decoration in many of their celebrations. Over time, holly has become a symbol of Christmas and so have its colors: red and green.

▲ Mistletoe, which stays green throughout the year, was considered sacred by the ancient Celts. The Celtic influence can be seen in the custom of hanging mistletoe during Christmas.

■ Customs

THE TREE TRANSPORTED

In the days before photography, television, telephones, and the Internet, it took longer for ideas to move from one place to another, and even longer for them to move from one country to another. For example, the idea of having a Christmas tree traveled slowly from Germany in the first half of the 700s to other European countries, and then finally to North America. In 1561, in northeastern

▲ In 1848 this illustration, drawn by J. L. Williams, appeared in the *London Illustrated News*, popularizing the Christmas tree in the United Kingdom and ultimately in North America.

France, the Forest Ordinance of Ammerschweier, Alsace stated, "No burgher shall have for Christmas more than one bush of more than eight shoes' length." (A burgher
was a citizen of a city or town.) From this rule it is known that people were putting up and probably decorating Christmas vegetation. The first time a tree is actually referred to as a Christmas tree also took place in Alsace, in 1604. For the next 200 years customs developed and spread through the increasingly interlinked world. By 1829 Christmas trees were very popular in England.

Enjoy a short video on the Christmas tree lighting in Rockefeller Center, New York City.

In 1835, a German immigrant and Harvard professor set up a tree for his son and two of his friends. He hung it with toys and placed wax candles on the branches. Harriet Martineau, a visiting writer from Britain, was there when the tree was revealed. (The early custom was to keep the tree hidden until fully decorated.) She wrote in her 1838 *Retrospect of Western Travel* that she had been "present at the introduction into the new country of the German Christmas-tree." She predicted "the Christmas-tree will become one of the most flourishing exotics of New-England." Though the tree she saw was not actually the first in the country, glowing descriptions such as hers helped increase the desire for having one.

By 1848, markets in Philadelphia had them for sale, but in much of North America they were still a rarity and sometimes even considered too pagan. It was an illustration that appeared in the *London Illustrated News* in that same year that truly launched the Christmas tree not only in the United Kingdom but also in North America, where an adaptation was later published. A full-page picture showed the British royal family around their tree at Windsor castle. It was a scene of domestic happiness and calm. The article that accompanied the picture described the tree in great detail, including the decorations, the gifts under the tree, and a description of when the tree was put up and taken down. Two years later, an almost identical picture showed up in the United States in *Godey's Lady's Book*. The artist had "Americanized" the original illustration by removing all the royal insignia and the Prince's mustache. It captured the imagination of the public in the United States, just as it had in England—only, of course, they thought it showed a typical American Christmas.

The original Christmas tree decorations were simple and made of materials such as sweets, fruits, berries, and gingerbread cookies. Candles were probably introduced as decorations in the late 18th century. By the 1850s, European decorations had already become quite elaborate. English author Charles Dickens described a tree covered not only with fruit and candy but also with dolls, miniature furniture, tiny musical instruments, and toy guns and swords. While the European decorations were becoming more and more ornate, North American Christmas trees were still being decorated with natural materials such as popcorn, paper flowers, and homemade dolls. Today one may still find natural or homemade ornaments, but most North American families rely on stores for their decorations, visiting department stores that may feature a group of trees decorated according to different "themes" and adorned with sets of ornaments in colors selected to go together. Technology also plays a part, especially as outdoor decorations have become increasingly showy. On front lawns and on the exteriors of homes, fabulous, timed light displays create magical effects and entire neighborhoods can transform with holiday lights. Statuary and mechanized lawn gnomes in the form of favorite Christmas personalities are also popular, reflecting how the holiday changes according to time and place.

Artificial trees first appeared in Germany in the 1800s and were made of wire and feathers. Germany was also the country that for many years made the most spectacular Christmas ornaments. Using a special process of hand-blowing glass into molds, artists made the insides of the ornaments look silvery. At first this effect came from mercury or lead. Later ornaments got their mirror-like surface from a special compound of silver nitrate and sugar water. The reflection of candles or electric lights off the ornament multiplied the magical glimmer.

The decorations people use on the top of their Christmas trees can be very symbolic. Some people choose an angel, in remembrance of the angel who appeared before Mary to tell her she would give birth to Jesus. A star is another popular symbol, representing the star seen by the three kings, as well as the idea of Christ as "the light of the world."

GIANT LANTERNS

Parols—star-shaped lanterns made out of bamboo, wire, and paper—are a popular Christmas decoration in the Philippines. The *parols* made in and around Manila, the capital of the Philippines, often contain real or imitation *capiz* shells. The shells are named after the province of the Philippines where they are often found. Other materials for *parols* include crepe paper, soft drink straws, glass, metal, and Japanese rice paper. Some *parols* are as large as 40 feet across. Since lantern making became a small industry in the 1970s, it has provided employment for 10,000 families. It is also a strong draw for tourists during the Christmas season.

▲ Today, Christmas trees are popular decorations in many countries. Shown here is the Rockefeller Center Christmas tree in New York City.

SING WE ALL NOËL

One of the oldest Christmas customs is the singing of carols. As one might expect, singing at festivals is a custom probably as old as the festivals themselves. The word *carol* or *carole* probably came from French or Anglo-Saxon–the language spoken by ancient tribes who entered Britain. Originally carols were meant to accompany dancing, and they usually dealt with religious subjects. For about 200 years, carols enjoyed great popularity. Then, in the 1600s they almost disappeared. It was not until a revived interest in Christmas during the early 1800s, attributed to the popularity of written works such as Charles Dickens's novel *A Christmas Carol*, Clement Clarke Moore's poem "Twas the Night Before Christmas," and Washington Irving's short story "Old Christmas," that carols finally came out of hibernation. In 1833 a book of more than 200 carols was published. In current times, most people consider a carol any song that celebrates Christmas, whether it has a religious theme or not.

In addition to certain beloved carols and the Christmas tree, the Advent calendar originated in Germany at least as early as the 19th century. In its simplest version, the calendar consists of two layers of paper glued together. Numbered doors are cut into the front piece of paper and colorful illustrations are placed on the page behind it. Each illustration has to line up in such a way that when the door in front of it is opened,

TALLYING "THE TWELVE DAYS OF CHRISTMAS"

Every year PNC Wealth Management figures out what it would cost to buy all the items mentioned in the song, "The Twelve Days of Christmas" (12 drummers drumming, 11 pipers piping, 10 lords a leaping, nine ladies dancing, eight maids a milking, seven swans a swimming, six geese a laying, five golden rings, four calling birds, three French hens, two turtle doves, and a partridge in a pear tree). They check with jewelry stores, dance companies, pet stores, and other sources to come up with their results. According to their calculations, at 2016 prices, buying each item in the song once would cost $34,363. It would cost $156,508 to buy the number of objects accumulated after 12 days–a whopping 364–because of all the repeats. Some things cost the same as they did the previous year (three French hens: $181.50; four calling birds: $599.96). However, the two turtledoves spiked in price by almost 30 percent, due to their high demand. The index has been calculated since 1984.

▲ In front of the Brandenburg Gate in Berlin, Germany, a large Christmas tree is decorated each year. During the Christmas season, carolers walk the streets in Germany, singing and collecting money for charitable causes.

the picture is clearly visible. Each number corresponds to a day in the "countdown" to Christmas. A child opens the door labeled "1" on the first day of December. Behind the door there is usually an illustration of something related to Christmas—such as a candle, a tree, or a toy. Although the idea is simple, Advent calendars have delighted children for more than 150 years. The Advent calendar probably began with a simple chalk mark used to count the days before Christmas. Later, people began to light a candle each night, or to put up a tiny religious picture each day.

German Gerhad Lang, who created the first printed Advent calendars in 1908, got the idea from a childhood ritual begun by his mother. She attached tiny candles to a piece of cardboard and each day he would remove one as Christmas approached. Lang's first Advent calendars were printed with numbered pictures. Several years later he introduced calendars with 24 little doors like the ones children enjoy today.

During World War II (1939–45), Advent calendars were discontinued, probably to save paper. Once the war was over, production of them resumed. Some clever three-dimensional calendars have taken the idea of the Advent calendar one step further. These calendars have numbered pockets and inside each pocket a treat or toy is hidden.

■ The Arrival of Santa Claus

Giving gifts is very much a part of modern Christmas festivities. The practice may have originated with Saturnalia, when it was common to exchange gifts. Christians also view gift-giving as an echo of the gifts given to Jesus by the three magi, the three wise men who traveled to Bethlehem in search of a newborn king. Originally Christmas gifts were much simpler than they are today. Children in 19th-century Europe or North America typically received red rubber balls, boxes of colored pencils, and, perhaps, a dollar or two from their grandparents. Many gifts were homemade, not only because mass-produced items did not exist, but few people could afford to spend much on them. Today, the commercial element of Christmas is a major driver of Western economies. For many in the United States, the day after Thanksgiving marks the beginning of Christmas shopping. It has been nicknamed "Black Friday" because retailers

THE REAL ST. NICHOLAS

The Roman Catholic Church has permitted one scientific analysis of bones belonging to Saint Nicholas, which lie in the town of Bari in southern Italy. In the late 1950s, when the chapel was being restored, a special group of scientists was allowed to photograph and measure the contents of the grave. Using computer-generated facial reconstruction, X-rays, and precise measurements, a laboratory in England revealed new information about what Saint Nicholas actually looked like. The data showed that he was barely five feet tall (which was shorter than average, even for the time in which he lived), and had a broken nose.

▲ A child shares his list of presents with Father Christmas in Ukraine.

turn profitable for the year from sales made on this day, and black in accounting practice is used to show a positive balance (red denotes negative).

The identity of who is believed to bring the gifts varies by culture, as does the day on which gifts are received. In countries that are mostly Protestant, such as the United States, Canada, England, and Australia, children ask Santa Claus to fulfill their Christmas wishes. In countries in which most of the Christians are Catholic, it is the three kings who bring the gifts to children, just as they brought gifts to the baby Jesus. In the European countries where populations follow Eastern Orthodox traditions, Saint Nicholas brings gifts on his feast day of December 6.

Santa Claus's Christian origins are evident in his name as well as in the red and white costume he wears, which has similarities to the robes worn by a bishop of the church. The tradition of asking children about their behavior is also a custom associated with Saint Nicholas. (A child will only receive Christmas presents if he or she has been well behaved during the year.)

Christian families in most European countries exchange gifts on December 24, often after attending mass. In North America, the morning of December 25 is the time for opening gifts, perhaps because of the strong influence of the poem "A Visit from St. Nicholas," more popularly known as "The Night Before Christmas." As a result, Christians in North America usually attend church services on Christmas Eve. "Midnight" masses are offered by a great number of churches, even though mass may not start at midnight.

There are several stories about the origins of Santa Claus, but some see an inspiration in a real-life bishop from the third century who lived in what is now Turkey. After he was credited for performing astonishing miracles, Saint Nicholas became known as Nicholas the Wonderworker. His popularity gradually spread throughout Europe. Unlike the plump, rosy-cheeked Santa Claus so familiar today, Saint Nicholas was usually shown as a tall, thin man, dressed in robes and wearing a pointed bishop's *mitre*, or hat, on his head. In paintings he often appeared clasping a gospel book, assisted by one or more African pageboys known as Black Pete. He is the patron saint of children, orphans, and students, due to his love for them—as well as for his kindness and generosity. He is also the patron saint of sailors, fishermen, the falsely accused, and various people who have behaved badly but have asked for forgiveness. He is one of the most popular Christian saints in the world. In fact, he is the patron saint of numerous countries, including Greece, Russia, Germany, Austria, and Belgium.

THE CHRISTMAS STORY

For many people, celebrating Christmas means turning their attention to stories and **reenactments** of Jesus' life. Four of Jesus' followers wrote books in which they recorded events in his life, as well as his teachings. These are known as the gospels. The Christmas story as it is known today comes mostly from the gospels of Matthew and Luke. The gospels of Matthew and Luke were written years after Jesus' death. They emphasize different aspects of the story and disagree on some of the details. The gospels of Mark and John include no mention of Jesus' birth and childhood. Since there were no eyewitnesses who can confirm or deny the stories, many questions of historical accuracy remain unanswered. Luke's version is the most popular, but it does not include the visit by the three wise men, later described as three kings. The story that is reenacted annually around the world combines elements from both Luke's version and Matthew's.

Like other religions, Christianity has angels. According to the gospel of Luke, the archangel Gabriel appeared to Mary, who was engaged to wed Joseph. Gabriel told Mary that she was carrying God's child, even though she was a virgin. Joseph and Mary married soon afterward. Joseph was a carpenter from Nazareth, and descended from the line of the second king of Israel, David, both through his father, Jacob, and because he was the adopted son of Heli, who was also descended from David. Joseph and Mary traveled to Bethlehem to enroll in the **census**

▲ Residents of Nazareth playing the roles of Mary, holding the baby Jesus, and Joseph, reenact the nativity, the birth of Jesus Christ. This scene is in Nazareth Village, a model of a first-century Galilean village in the Arab town of Nazareth in northern Israel.

▲ The three magi, or wise men, greet citizens and visitors in Barcelona, Spain, on January 6 to celebrate the feast of the **Epiphany**. The Christian feast of the Epiphany recalls the magi's journey to visit the infant Jesus.

(a population count) that had been ordered by the Roman emperor Augustus. Since so many other people were in Bethlehem at the same time, Mary and Joseph could not find an inn in which to sleep. They took refuge in a stable, where Jesus was born.

In the gospel of Matthew, three magi, or wise men, came to Bethlehem guided by a bright star. "Where is he who has been born king of the Jews? For we have seen his star in the East, and have come to worship him." (Matthew 2:2) It is not known how the magi traveled. They are often pictured riding camels, though they may have walked. The magi attracted the interest of King

Herod I, who was king of Judaea (now southern Israel). As one might imagine, King Herod found their talk of a new king threatening. He obtained from the magi information about where Jesus was to be found, but not the specific location. He asked them to discover the site and report back to him.

The three magi eventually arrived at the stable and presented Jesus with gifts of "frankincense, gold, and myrrh." (Frankincense and myrrh are dried tree saps, or resins, that are burned as incense, often after being mixed with herbs and spices.) During the night, each magi dreamt that Herod wanted to murder the child to protect his kingship. As a result, they returned home without reporting to Herod the location of the stable.

Even though the kings appear only in Matthew's version, their inclusion in the story quickly became popular. Over time, it was expanded on and made more elaborate. As early as the third century, the magi were considered kings instead of wise men, probably to fit with the prophecy in Psalms 72:11: "May all kings fall down before him."

Saint Francis Assisi of Italy is given credit for turning the nativity, the birth of Jesus, into a three-dimensional scene on Christmas Eve 1223. According to his biographer, the Franciscan friar Thomas of Celano (ca. 1200–ca. 1270), Saint Francis set up a real straw-filled manger between an ox and a donkey, then held Christmas Mass on the manger.

During Christmas, many Christians set up a small replica of the nativity scene in their homes. In French-speaking countries, and in areas such as French Canada (Quebec) and the Creole sections of Louisiana, all churches and many homes display such a scene. They call it a crèche, which means manger–the trough that usually holds grains for horses or cows. In Spanish-speaking countries, it is known as the *nacimiento*, which means birth. In Mexico, as in many other countries, the figure of Baby Jesus is not placed in the scene until Christmas Eve.

TEXT-DEPENDENT QUESTIONS

1: Where is the town of Nazareth?

2: What British writer described the early custom of the Christmas tree in 1838?

3: What is an Advent calendar, and when were the first printed Advent calendars produced?

RESEARCH PROJECTS

1: Select a famous Christmas carol. Research its history, writer(s) and composer(s), and the story behind its creation. Write a brief report summarizing your findings.

2: Research the history of the nativity play or Christmas pageant, in which participants reenact roles in the story of Christ's birth. Write a brief report detailing the characters of the play, how the play functions, and some facts about the history of its performance.

▲ A church choir performs traditional Christmas carols for shoppers at a mall in Great Britain.

Origins of Hanukkah

■ A Celebration of History

Since Hanukkah often takes place around December, some non-Jews assume that Hanukkah is similar to Christmas in the Christian Church. In fact, it is quite different. Christmas began as a religious holiday, but Hanukkah is rooted in an event of historical and cultural importance for Jews. Hanukkah is probably the Jewish holiday best documented in historical sources, although it does not appear in the Torah, the Jewish holy scriptures.

WORDS TO UNDERSTAND

Blintze: A thin pancake that is usually folded to enclose fillings such as ricotta cheese or fruit, and then baked or sautéed.

Depict: To represent with an image or illustration.

Gregorian calendar: The most commonly used calendar internationally, which was introduced in 1582 by Pope Gregory XIII.

Hellenism: A group of values and philosophies that originated in ancient Greece.

◀ Hannukah celebrates the miracle of one day's worth of oil lasting for eight days to keep the sacred lights burning.

After the Greek conqueror Alexander the Great took over Syria (which in ancient times was the whole fertile strip between the eastern Mediterranean and the desert of northern Arabia), Egypt, and Palestine, he allowed the people of the region to continue their religious practices. But Alexander died in 323 B.C.E. After Alexander's death, his three generals–Antigonus, Seleucus, and Ptolemy–fought over his kingdom. Antigonus eventually ended up with Greece and Macedonia (on the northern border of Greece); Ptolemy got rulership of Israel and Egypt; and Seleucus took charge of Babylonia (now southern Iraq), Persia (today's Iran), and Syria.

▲ Ptolemy, who ruled Israel and Egypt after the death of Alexander the Great, was in favor of Greek nationalism, also known as Hellenism.

Ptolemy was in favor of Greek nationalism, which was also known as **Hellenism**, so he favored having everything done according to the Greek tradition. During Ptolemy's rule, many Jews adopted Greek dress and the Greek language. Many Jews thought that the best way to succeed in Greek society was to blend in with the culture that surrounded them. Nevertheless, they maintained their religious identity. The Jews believed in one god, while the Greeks worshipped a number of gods.

SPELLING A HEBREW WORD IN ENGLISH

People around the world often wonder about the correct spelling of *Hanukkah*. Here are some of the spelling variations: Chanuka, Chanukkah, Hanuka, Hanukka, Hanaka, Haneka, Hanika, Khanukkah. The variety arises from using the Roman alphabet to spell a word from Hebrew, a language that has a completely different alphabet.

▲ A rabbi stands behind a menorah that is used to help celebrate the eight days of Hanukkah in San Bernardino, California.

The Jews' religious freedom in Jerusalem continued into the next century. While other cities were encouraged to adopt Greek culture and politics, Jerusalem's high priest continued to rule according to Jewish law. The military stationed in Jerusalem were the only non-Jews in the city. By 175 B.C.E., however, King Antiochus IV had become the ruler of Syria. In the Book of Daniel in the Tanakh, or Hebrew Bible, Antiochus is described as a conqueror and a man of great arrogance and pride. When he took over, he inherited a kingdom whose treasury had been drained by years of war and conquest. Like the previous king, he was desperate for money. Antiochus was also a great admirer of Greek culture, just as the previous king had been. He thought that the best way to expand his kingdom was to turn all the cities he conquered into Greek cities, and to force all conquered people to follow the Greek religion.

At that time in Jerusalem, there were two main parties of Jews: the Hasideans and a party that favored reform and Hellenistic ideas. Because the Hellenistic Jews were wealthier than the Hasideans, they had an easier time influencing the king. The high priest's brother, Jason, belonged to the Hellenistic group. He offered to pay the king a large sum of money in exchange for being appointed high priest. He agreed to pay even more if Antiochus would let him set up "a gymnasium and a training place for the youth and to enroll the people of Jerusalem as citizens of Antioch." (II Macc. 3:7) Antiochus agreed, and Jason's brother was stripped of his title and arrested. Antiochus's actions outraged the Jews who opposed Hellenization. Normally, someone only became high priest when the previous priest died. Also, they were furious that the king had interfered in their religious matters.

No one knows if Jason planned for only his followers to become Greek citizens, or whether he wanted every Jew in Jerusalem to become a Greek citizen. What is known is that he had a gymnasium and school modeled on the Greek system built at the northern edge of the Jewish temple. It included a library and became a cultural meeting place. According to the account in the Book of Maccabees, the priests from the temple started to spend time at the wrestling school when they should have been in the temple performing their duties. Whereas before Jerusalem had maintained its Jewish character, under Jason it started to become like the other cities that had adopted Greek ways.

CIVIL WAR

For three years, Jason continued as high priest. During this time, the conflicts between the Hellenistic Jews and the conservative Hasideans continued to rise, resulting in what was essentially civil war. However, in 170 B.C.E., while Antiochus was off fighting in Egypt, Jason sent a priest named

Menelaus to pay Antiochus the usual tribute (a payment made usually by a state or ruler to another, often as a sign of dependence). This was a big mistake. Menelaus was not only more radical about Hellenism than was Jason, he was willing to pay a bigger bribe to Antiochus in exchange for being high priest. Antiochus saw this as an offer too good to refuse, so Menelaus returned to Jerusalem and became high priest. Jason left the city in defeat, while Menelaus worked even harder to turn Jerusalem into a Greek city.

In 168 B.C.E. a false rumor spread to the people of Jerusalem. They heard that Antiochus had been killed during his second invasion of Egypt. They believed they were suddenly leaderless. Each side (both the Hasideans and the Hellenistic Jews) wanted to be sure that they

▲ This frieze from the Arch of Titus in Rome shows the principal symbol of Hanukkah, the seven-branched candelabra known as a *menorah*. The carving depicts Romans–the successors to the Greeks in Palestine–sacking the Second Temple of Jerusalem in 70 C.E.

▲ Members of the Jewish community come together with their children at the beginning of the Hanukkah festival in Madrid, Spain.

would get control of the city, so they split into factions, or different groups, and began fighting in the streets. Jason, who had never accepted losing his position of high priest, saw this as a way to regain his post, even if he had to use force. He marched on Jerusalem with nearly 1,000 supporters. At first it looked as if he would win, but eventually he was forced to retreat, and fled to Egypt.

In the meantime, Antiochus was actually very much alive. He was not, however, in a peaceful mood. His first invasion of Egypt had been successful, but his second was not. When he tried to take over the city of Alexandria, the Romans stopped him. Though not directly involved, the Romans considered Egypt under their protection. They threatened to go to war against Antiochus if he did not leave immediately. The king was forced to retreat in frustration.

When Antiochus got news of the fighting in Jerusalem, he did not realize that the Jews were fighting each other for control of the city. He believed that the city was in revolt against his authority. He responded by returning with his large army of troops and taking the city by storm. Many people were killed. Others were captured and sold as slaves.

After this incident, Antiochus outlawed Jewish rituals and burned any copies of the laws of Moses (the Torah) that he could find. He forbade the Jews to observe the Sabbath or any of their traditional feasts and holy days. In the beginning, a number of Jews went along with the king's commands. However, on December 25, 167 B.C.E., Antiochus seized the temple in Jerusalem and dedicated it to the worship of Zeus, the mightiest of the Greek gods. By his desecration, or disrespect, for the temple that the Jews considered holy, Antiochus lost the support of all Jews.

TAKING BACK THE TEMPLE

The turning point in the conflict between the king and the Jews took place in the village of Modi'in, not far from Jerusalem. A Greek officer and his soldiers ordered villagers to bow down to an idol (a representation or symbol of an object of worship) and to accept the sacrifice of pigs on the altar, activities forbidden to Jews. When the officer told

A HANUKKAH SONG: MI Y'MALEIL

**Who can retell the things that befell them,
Who can count them?
In every age, a hero or sage
came to our aid.
Hark! In days of yore
In Israel's ancient land,
Brave Maccabeus led the faithful band.
But now all Israel must as one arise,
Redeem itself through deed and sacrifice.**

Mattathias, the high priest of the village, to take part in the ceremony, he refused. When another Jew stepped forward and agreed to obey the officer's order, Mattathias became enraged. He took out his sword and killed both the Jew and the Greek officer. Then he, his five sons, and some other villagers attacked and killed the rest of the group of soldiers. Mattathias then went into hiding in the mountains, along with his family and those Jews who wanted to fight alongside him. The result was a full-blown rebellion of the Jews against the Greeks.

Mattathias died about a year after the rebellion began. His third son, Judas Maccabeus, became the leader of the resistance. Finally in December, three years after Antiochus had conquered Jerusalem in 167 B.C.E., Judas Maccabeus recaptured most of it. Maccabeus regained all that had been taken except for the fortress Antiochus had built on the hill above the Temple. Judas then had priests cleanse the Temple and put up an altar of rough stones. They set to work to rededicate the holy space.

The Hebrew word *Hanukkah* means "dedication." According to the records, there was very little oil left for use in the Temple. The priests needed oil to light the menorah, or candelabra, which was supposed to burn constantly and never go out. They finally found enough oil to light the menorah, but only enough for one day. Miraculously, the oil burned not for one night but for eight, long enough for the Maccabees to prepare fresh oil for the menorah.

■ Hanukkah Customs

While in the past Hanukkah was not a holiday of great religious importance to the Jews, its significance has grown for a variety of reasons. Jews of the latter 20th century may observe Hanukkah because they can, and because they feel a responsibility to the victims of genocide (murder) against Jews. Others appreciate the essential symbolic elements of Hanukkah: that as one candle lights another, so might the light of compassion move between people, as the wish is worded in a popular interpretation.

Jewish families in the West may also feel forced to make a greater show of the holiday so they do not get swept away by the dominant Christian culture. Some Jewish children receive Hanukkah gifts on a par with Christmas giving, although traditionally Hanukkah gifts consisted mainly of little treats. Often members of the Jewish community hold special events so that each family can be part of a larger celebration. Los Angeles, California, for example, has a Hanukkah Family Festival. The festival includes a number of Hanukkah-related activities, such as art workshops, storytelling, sampling holiday treats, and taking time to light Hanukkah candles and remember the importance of having religious freedom.

▲ Cities across the U.S. hold special events for the lighting of the menorah. This menorah is in West Palm Beach, Florida.

People of all faiths look to examples of courage when confronted with prejudice or persecution. Martyrs, or people who face torture or death for holding onto their beliefs, make up a significant part of the history of Hanukkah. The most famous martyr is a woman named Hannah. She and her seven sons were arrested and brought before King Antiochus IV of Syria. In some versions they were commanded to eat pork, in others to bow before idols—both forbidden by Jewish law. When Hannah and her sons refused, the king had her eldest son killed in front of her, hoping that the sight would convince the others to give in. They did not, however. The king ordered each son killed, one after the other, and finally Hannah herself was murdered. During periods when Jews have suffered terrible treatment and sometimes death, they looked to martyrs such as Hannah as role models to help them endure.

WHEN TO CELEBRATE HANUKKAH

Of the five major solar calendars in use today, the **Gregorian calendar** is the one that's most widely used. For religious observance, however, Jews follow their own calendar. The Jewish calendar, like the Gregorian calendar, has seven days in a week and 12 months in a year, but in Judaism, a day begins at sundown.

The festival of Hanukkah begins on the 25th day of Kislev. This is the name of the ninth month of the Jewish calendar. The Hanukkah festival goes to the second of Tevet, the 10th month of the Jewish calendar. As a result, Hanukkah does not begin on the same day every year. It usually begins in what is middle or late December in the Gregorian calendar. Though established as a religious holiday, today both Jews and non-Jews often participate in the rituals as celebrations have moved to public squares, especially in the cities of Europe where historically Jews have been vilified (treated as a villain) and persecuted. These outward changes are seen by many as wondrous proof of the power of the human spirit and humankind to adapt and grow.

JEWISH AND GREGORIAN CALENDAR EQUIVALENTS

Month	Days	Gregorian
Nisan	30	March-April
Iyyar	29	April-May
Sivan	30	May-June
Tammuz	29	June-July
Av	30	July-August
Elul	29	August-September
Tishri	30	September-October
Cheshvan	29/30	October-November
Kislev	30/29	November-December
Tevet	29	December-January
Shevat	30	January-February
Adar	29/30	February-March

▲ From the traditional to the modern, the variety of menorahs reflects the diversity of Jewish observance.

Many of the customs relating to Hanukkah are described in the Talmud, a historical religious book that contains the discussions and decisions made by Jewish religious leaders about Jewish law and ethics. (The first part of the Talmud was written in 200 C.E.) According to the Talmud, the special menorah of Hanukkah, called the *hanukkiyah*, must hold nine candles, one for each of the eight nights that the oil burned in the Temple in Jerusalem as well as a *shamash*, or servant candle. The *shamash* is used to light the other candles, and may not be used for any other purpose. The lights are also to burn for at least a half hour after it gets dark outside.

The first night of Hanukkah, one candle is placed to the far right. Participants recite three blessings, and then the *shamash* candle is used to light the first candle. The candle is allowed to burn out on its own. Each night another candle is added, from right to left. After the first night, only the first two blessings are recited before the lighting of the candles. On the eighth night, all nine candles–the *shamash* candle and the eight Hanukkah candles–are lit. Oil lamps can be used in place of candles, and electric lights are sometimes used where an open flame would be dangerous.

Once lit, the *hanukkiyah* should be placed where everyone can see it, such as in a window near the street, as emblem of Judaism's survival. Jews do not need to observe this rule, however, if lighting the candles might endanger the lives of the Jews within the house, such as during a time of religious persecution.

SYMBOLIC FOODS FOR HANUKKAH

Because of the role that oil plays in the holiday, it is customary to eat foods fried in oil on Hanukkah. Ashkenazi Jews–the Jews that descended from the medieval Jews of Eastern Europe, literally "German Jews"–typically make and eat latkes, or fried potato pancakes. These delightful mouthfuls made from potato strips, egg, and onion are usually served with applesauce and sour cream. The original latkes were made with some combination of vegetables, cheese, and fruit (at the time, potatoes had not been introduced to the Middle East). Sephardic Jews–the Jews who left Spain and Portugal to escape persecution–customarily make jelly doughnuts known as *soofganiyot*, or they cook fritters, small masses of fried batter, in syrup known as *zalabia*. Other favorite foods for Hanukkah include beef brisket, chopped liver, cucumber salad with dill and applesauce, shortbread cookies in the shape of menorahs and dreidels, fruit strudel, and noodle *kuchen*–a type of German coffee cake. Often Jews and non-Jews gather together during Hanukkah to enjoy these special foods.

At family gatherings, European Jews who have been influenced by living with Christians generally serve roast goose, whereas Jews in Italy and Morocco often serve deep-fried chicken. In Russia and Poland people enjoy *borscht*, a hearty beet soup topped with sour cream, as part of their Hanukkah menu.

Sephardic Jews commonly serve dairy foods as well as fried foods. These may be cheesecakes, or **blintzes** (a thin pancake stuffed with ricotta or fruit), topped with sour cream or cottage cheese. These are prepared in memory of Judith, a Jewish widow who, according to some stories, saved her town from an invading general. The general and his troops were planning to conquer the town. Judith convinced him to consume so much wine and cheese that he fell asleep. She then killed him as he slept. Historians may not agree on these events, but the custom of eating dairy foods during Hanukkah honors her courage.

▲ Golden-fried potato latkes served with apple sauce are a traditional Hanukkah food for Ashkenazi or Eastern European Jews.

■ The Dreidel Tradition

One of the traditions of Hanukkah is the game of dreidel (*s'vivon* in Hebrew), a game in which each player spins a four-sided square top. The dreidel is marked with four Hebrew letters: nun, gimel, hei, and shin. Some rabbis (teachers of Jewish law and

Learn some of the basic rules of playing the game of dreidel.

custom) believe the letters stand for the Hebrew sentence *Nes gadol hayah sham*, or "A great miracle happened there," referring to the miracle of the oil. In modern Israel, the letters have been changed to reflect the translation "A great miracle happened *here*."

Most people play for matchsticks, pennies, or chocolate Hanukkah *gelt* (*gelt* is the Yiddish word for "money"). The letters have meanings in Yiddish, as well as Hebrew. Yiddish is the language of the Ashkenazi Jews. They use *nit* (nothing), *gantz* (all), *halb* (half), and *shtell* (put).

▲ Dreidels are traditional toys that teach Jewish children the meaning of Hanukkah while they play.

Depending on which side the top lands, the player takes different actions. If the top lands on nun, nothing happens. If it lands on gimel, the player gets the whole pot. Half the pot is awarded if the dreidel lands on hei, and if it lands on shin, the player puts in a penny or whatever he or she is using to count. When the pot is empty, everyone puts one counter in. Everyone keeps playing until one person has all the counters. The Jewish dreidel game is most likely based on the German equivalent called *totum*. In German, N = *nichts* = nothing; G = *ganz* = all; H = *halb* = half; and S = *stell ein* = put in.

One 19th-century rabbi explained the connection between the dreidel and Hanukkah by saying that the Jews played with the dreidel to fool the Greeks. The Greeks had forbidden them to study the Torah. Since playing with the dreidel was legal and studying the Torah was not, the Jews pretended to be playing to disguise their reading of the Torah. In fact, the dreidel originally had no connection to Hanukkah at all. A similar game that involved using a top was played in many cultures for centuries. In England and Ireland, a game called *teetotum* or *totum* was commonly played around Christmastime. By 1801, in England the four letters T, H, P, and N appeared on the sides of the top, representing Take all, Half, Put down, and Nothing.

A HANUKKAH SONG: I HAVE A LITTLE DREIDEL

I have a little dreidel,
I made it out of clay.
And when it's dry and ready,
Oh dreidel I shall play.
(Chorus)
Oh dreidel, dreidel, dreidel,
I made it out of clay;
And when it's dry and ready,
Then dreidel I shall play.
It has a lovely body,
With legs so short and thin.
And when it gets all tired,
It drops and then I win.
(Chorus)

▲ The lighting of the menorah is celebrated by the whole family.

 **TEXT-DEPENDENT QUESTIONS**

1: Who became the ruler of Syria in 175 B.C.E.?

2: What does the Hebrew word *Hanukkah* mean?

3: Name three foods traditionally served during Hanukkah.

RESEARCH PROJECTS

1: Research some of the similarities and differences between Ashkenazi and Sephardic Jews, including regional histories, customs, devotional practices, and other cultural elements. Write a brief report comparing and contrasting the two groups.

2: Research some of the history, components, and religious purposes of the Talmud, including the difference between the Mishnah and Gemara. Write a brief report introducing the Talmud to a general audience.

▲ Doughnuts, which are fried in oil, are a traditional Hanukkah treat symbolizing the miracle of the oil in the temple lasting for eight days.

European Traditions and Customs

Europe today is predominantly Christian and has been for nearly 2,000 years—since the time of the Roman Empire. In creating their own holidays, early Christians often looked to existing pagan holidays. This was certainly the case in Europe. From Christmas trees to Father Christmas, many of the traditions taken for granted today were adopted from much earlier, pre-Christian festivals.

As well as being the seat of Christianity, Europe has an old and established Jewish identity. From Russia and Eastern Europe to Germany, England, France, and Spain, Jewish communities made great contributions to European culture. An example of the

WORDS TO UNDERSTAND

Amidst: In the middle of.

Fast: The practice of not eating or not eating certain foods for a period of time.

Longstanding: That which has lasted a long time.

Superstition: A belief of cause and effect that is not founded on rationality or proof. For example, the belief that wearing red socks will make a student do well on a test could be considered a superstition.

◀ King Ferdinand and Queen Isabella of Spain ordered all Jews to convert to Christianity or be expelled from the country. The monarchs are shown here meeting with Christopher Columbus, whose voyage they funded.

▲ Swiss villagers dance with their *iffelen*, which are artfully designed giant *mitres* lit by candles from within during the traditional Klausjagen procession held each December 5. The ancient custom of Klausjagen, or Saint Nicholas hunt, where villagers accompany Saint Nicholas through the village, is a Christian celebration with pagan roots that go back to the Middle Ages.

contribution they made became evident after 1492, when King Ferdinand and Queen Isabella of Spain ruled that all Jews must convert to Christianity or be expelled from the country. (These were the same rulers who sponsored Christopher Columbus.) Although Ferdinand and Isabella–known as the "Catholic Kings"–helped stabilize their country's political situation, their lack of religious tolerance led to the Spanish Inquisition, a period of persecution during which 3,000 to 5,000 people died for not being Catholic.

In 1492, Jews occupied positions in all levels of society. Notable Jews of the time were diplomats, financial advisors, poets, philosophers, mathematicians, physicians, astronomers, statesmen, explorers, and scientists, just to name a few. When Ferdinand and Isabella expelled the Jews, Spain lost some of the brightest and most creative minds of the era. While the Jews who left Spain and Portugal became known as Sephardic Jews, today the term is also applied to Jews who worship in Sephardic temples and follow Sephardic traditions.

Another large exodus (mass departure) of Jews took place when the ugly and extreme fear of Jews that gripped Europe in the 1930s and 1940s culminated in the Holocaust. Six million European Jews were systematically murdered, and following World War II (1939-1945), many survivors moved to other parts of the world. The Jews who descended from the medieval Jews of Eastern Europe are called Ashkenazi, literally "German Jews." Currently, about 80 percent of the world's Jews are Ashkenazi.

Today Europe's Jewish population is healing and growing. Many towns throughout Europe now display a menorah in the town square, right next to the Christmas tree. In addition, many more people around the world have become familiar with Hanukkah and other Jewish holidays, thanks to increased global communication and the Internet.

■ Christmas in France

France is an overwhelmingly Christian country. Of the almost 64 million residents, Roman Catholics and Protestants make up close to 90 percent of the population.

Christmas celebrations begin on December 24, Christmas Eve, in France, and they end on December 26. On Christmas Eve, families often go to church together. They usually attend Midnight Mass, which is a tradition unique to Christmas. Later the families have a large meal at home or in a café or restaurant. These last two generally stay open late in France throughout the entire year. People make and enjoy delicacies as part of this celebration.

The Christmas tree is known as *le sapin de Noël*. As in so many other countries where Christmas is celebrated, it is a decoration seen everywhere—inside the home, in stores, and as public decorations. Christmas markets also thrive in France. The oldest one is in Strasbourg, and runs from the last week in November to Christmas Eve. The market is set in front of the beautiful Strasbourg cathedral, so anyone bored with shopping can sit and gaze at the delicate stone carving on the façade, and admire the jeweled colors of the stained glass windows.

On Christmas day, families usually have a special Christmas meal together. It generally includes some combination of

HANUKKAH IN FRANCE

Only about 1 percent of the French in France are Jewish, but that still amounts to approximately 640,000 people. People who celebrate Hanukkah in Paris can go to one of the restaurants that have created a new tradition of serving Hanukkah food.

turkey, goose, and chicken. For dessert, the Christmas specialty in France is *bûche de Noël*. This is a particularly rich cake that is shaped and decorated to look like a log of wood, such as one would put in a fireplace. The tradition comes from the pagan custom of the Yule log, which died away when gigantic open hearths were replaced by small iron stoves. The large logs gave way to small logs decorated with holly and greens used for centerpieces on the table. In time the French, whose cuisine is legendary, came up with the sweet dessert made to look like a log. The chocolate buttercream frosting on the outside is scraped to look like bark, and powdered sugar is sprinkled on top to resemble snow. For a finishing touch, these cakes are often decorated with fresh berries and meringue shaped to look like mushrooms.

Children receive gifts from Père Noël, their name for Father Christmas. A helper named Pre Fouettard accompanies him. It is Pre Fouettard's duty to tell Père Noël how each child has behaved during the past year. In some areas of France Père Noël distributes children's gifts on Saint Nicholas Eve (December 5). The adults generally exchange gifts on New Year's Day.

▲ Trees lining the Champs-Elysées Avenue in Paris, France, twinkle with white lights at Christmas.

▲ The Strasbourg Christmas market is one of the largest holiday markets in France.

The manger or crèche is the centerpiece around which most Christmas festivities take place in France. It is often filled with small clay figures called "little saints" (*stantons*). In the south of France these include replicas of local dignitaries and other local characters.

■ Christmas in Germany

Many Christmas customs North Americans celebrate came from Germany, as did the idea of Christmas as a time for family. In Germany, the Christmas holiday begins on December 24 and ends on December 26. Christmas Day is called *der erste Weihnachtsfeiertag*, or the first day of Christmas. If they have not attended Midnight Mass on Christmas Eve, German Christians go to mass on Christmas Day. After that, they celebrate the holiday with their friends and families. For Germans, a dish made from goose meat is a favorite part of their Christmas meal.

In Germany, Christmas Eve is a very busy day. People decorate their Christmas trees, often using apples, stars, painted nuts, lights or candles, spicy biscuits called Lebkuchen, and other kinds of ornaments. The Germans not only perfected the art of blown glass ornaments, they are probably responsible for inventing tinsel. The original tinsel was real silver, cut from very thin sheets.

Unfortunately, it tarnished too easily, so it was replaced by pewter, a mixture of metals that includes tin. The pewter wasn't very successful in resisting tarnish, either. Modern tinsel is made of metallic plastic, which is much less expensive, but also much lighter, so the tinsel does not drape over the tree the way the old metal tinsel did.

As was customary when Christmas trees first arrived in North America, in Germany the parents decorate the tree in a room that is closed off from the children. Only when all the ornaments are in place and the lights are lit are the children invited to see the tree. Germans also open the presents under the tree on Christmas Eve. In many homes, this is the time to tell familiar stories or to sing carols. The favorite foods for the evening's dinner include fish, apples, almonds, and other kinds of nuts.

The most famous Christmas carol in the world was written in German. It was composed in Austria, near the Austrian-German border by a priest named Father Josef Mohr on Christmas Eve in 1818. English speakers know it as "Silent Night," but its original title was "Stille Nacht." Although Father Mohr had written the poem, he had not yet set it to music. The church organ was apparently

▲ Christmas lights and festive decorations can be seen on houses in a German town.

▲ A German baker mixes dough for *stollen* cake, a classic German Christmas treat. They have been made for centuries from traditional recipes that include butter, sugar, wheat flour, milk, almonds, and lemons. Only about 150 bakeries in the Dresden district of Germany are allowed to produce these cakes at Christmas time.

not working that night, so the writer and a composer, Franz Gruber, worked the tune out on a guitar. The tune was finished in time to be performed at midnight Mass. The simple tune that Gruber composed is sung slightly differently today; Gruber himself wrote several different arrangements of it during his lifetime.

Because the Advent calendar originated in Germany, it is appropriate that in a German town named Gengenbach, the whole town hall becomes an Advent calendar every year. Gengenbach's town hall has 24 windows (because Advent follows a religious calendar, the period beginning four Sundays before Christmas ranges from 22 to 28 days). Every year artists, often children's book illustrators, are hired to paint a scene to go behind each window. People gather each evening to see the unveiling of the next window, starting on November 30. The town of Reith has a similar tradition, however theirs is a "walking calendar." Since they do not have 24 windows in one building, each evening a window in another building is opened to reveal the picture behind it.

■ Hanukkah in Germany

Up until the last part of the 19th century, Jews enjoyed a reasonably stable life in Germany. They tended to live in smaller towns and villages, unevenly distributed across the country. At the time, Germany was broken up into many small communities, each with its own rules. Because of the variations in these rules, Jews lived among the general population in some locations and in almost ghetto-like concentrations in others. Around 1815, the greatest number of German Jews lived in the east in territories that had once been part of Poland, and in the southwest, with slightly smaller populations sprinkled in between.

As is so often the case, when there is enough to go around, people tend to be more tolerant and less selfish. The Germans were no different. Just before 1873, Germany was enjoying economic expansion. The coming of the railway had allowed many families to move to the cities, closer to better schools and business opportunities. Liberal Jewish parents, especially in urban areas, preferred to send their children to integrated schools with both Jewish and non-Jewish students. They believed that the way to overcome prejudice was to have all the students learn and play together. Though their children might encounter discrimination, there were still many fields open to them, especially in academics or business.

Celebrations of Hanukkah of the time reflected a similar mood. They were times of great socializing, for getting together and entertaining friends and relatives. Both devout and non-practicing Jews were invited to share in the long, friendly discussions over the dinner table, or to listen to music, or exchange books. Community members in both the cities and the villages gave each other support and advice, particularly since they so often shared similar careers and interests.

German victories over France during the Franco-German (or Franco-Prussian) War led to a unified Germany under King William of Prussia, who was crowned in 1871. As a consequence, France had to compensate Germany for war damages. The result was an economic boom for Germany, during which the railway expanded and new construction grew very rapidly. It was also a time of speculation, or taking chances. Investors became caught up in the exciting prospect of getting rich very quickly without regard to risk. The economic boom turned into inflation (an economic state in which prices rise because goods are scarce, and the value of money goes down). In 1873, Germany's stock market crashed, as it later crashed in other countries. Seemingly overnight, the attitude toward the Jews changed, especially because at the same time, a strongly anti-Semitic (anti-Jewish) member was elected to the Reichstag, the representational body of the country.

It was a time of contradictions. Jews who succeeded in their chosen fields feared that their success would make them stand out, causing envy or jealousy in those who were less successful. Anti-Semites tried to restrict Jews from studying fields such as medicine and law. They even tried to pressure hospitals and clinics to only employ Christian doctors. Many Jews developed private practices as a way to get around the restrictions. Before this period, many Jews had thought of themselves as Germans first and Jews second. Afterward, as well as during the terrible years of the Holocaust yet to come, Jews reacted by drawing closer to their culture and religion. Emphasis within the Jewish community began to focus on being Jewish as a way of life.

Prior to events such as the crash of 1873 and the Nazis' attempt to wipe out the Jews, Hanukkah in Germany had been a fun but fairly minor holiday. As the Jews' struggle for freedom became a struggle for survival itself, Hanukkah and another holiday, Purim, grew in importance. Both holidays commemorate moments in history in which enemies of the Jews tried to destroy them. The stories of resistance took on a new perspective, becoming symbolic of courage and endurance in the face of seemingly impossible odds. This change in attitude quickly spread to Jews everywhere.

Today, an unexpected event is taking place in Germany. Germany has the fastest-growing Jewish population in the world. Some families who left for Israel during the dark times of the 20th century returned because they missed their German heritage and didn't feel at home in the climate and culture of the Middle East. A large number have also come from Russia, escaping anti-Semitism that still exists in the former Soviet Union and hoping for better lives. Young Jews from Western countries also arrive, drawn to the vibrant lifestyle of Berlin. In addition, the German government offers resettlement programs for Jews from Eastern Europe, partly to make amends for the Holocaust.

Ironically, the greatest friction within this new Germany is taking place between the Jews who are settling there now and those who remained in Germany after the war. Although the Nazis declared Germany "free of Jews" in 1943, in fact there were several thousand Jews hidden away or later released from the concentration camps. These Jews continued to speak German and to carry on their religious traditions. Many Russian newcomers lost their customs and sometimes their sense of Jewish identity after living so long under communism. As is so often the case during any transition, change can mean a bumpy road.

Generally, however, there is optimism among the Jews that they can work out their differences. A woman who left Kiev, the capital of the Ukraine, where she and her family were forced to practice their faith in secret, rejoices in customs many Jews take for granted. She is delighted to have a synagogue and a rabbi, for her children to relearn Jewish traditions, and to openly celebrate holidays such as Hanukkah and Passover. "Germany has given us this freedom to find ourselves at last," she tells a reporter from the *Boston Globe* (Nickerson 2009).

Christmas in Russia

After the 1917 Revolution, Christmas–along with all other religious celebrations–was banned throughout Russia. To keep some of the Christmas traditions alive, Russian Christians reinvented the New Year's holiday. They included a decorated fir tree in their New Year's celebrations and introduced a character called "Grandfather Frost." Known as "Ded Moroz," Grandfather Frost looked very much like the western "Santa Claus" or "Père Noël," except that he dressed in a blue suit. Ded Moroz was actually a character that existed in the pagan culture, several centuries earlier. He is Grandfather Frost, the Russian Spirit of Winter who brings gifts on New Year's. He is accompanied by Snyegurochka, the Snowmaiden, who helps to distribute the gifts.

The Christmas tree, or *Yolka*, is another tradition that was banned during the Soviet era. To keep the custom alive, people decorated New Year's trees instead. Ornaments were either very costly or unavailable, so family trees were trimmed with homemade decorations and fruit.

▲ The head of Russia's Orthodox Church conducts a Christmas liturgy in Moscow. Christmas falls on January 7 for Orthodox Christians in the Holy Land, Russia, and other Eastern Orthodox churches that use the old Julian calendar instead of the Gregorian, or Western, calendar adopted by Catholics and Protestants and commonly used in secular life around the world.

Yolka comes from a word that refers to a fir tree. Emperor Peter the Great introduced Russia to the custom of decorating Christmas trees after he visited Europe during the 1700s. For a time, Christmas as a religious holiday was all but forgotten in the Soviet Union. In fact, it was generally celebrated only in small villages, where the citizenry were far from the communist party leaders.

It was not until 75 years after the 1917 Revolution, in 1992, that Christmas was openly observed. Today, it is once again celebrated in grand fashion, with the faithful participating in an all-night mass in incense-filled cathedrals **amidst** the company of the painted icons of saints.

Thirteen days after Western Christmas, on January 7, the Russian Orthodox Church celebrates its Christmas, in accordance with the old Julian calendar. It is a day of both solemn ritual and joyous celebration. Prior to the day, Orthodox Russians observe six weeks of vegetarian fasting. They do not attend parties or social gatherings, and they refrain from eating meat.

Christmas Eve, in the Russian tradition on January 6, is one of the highlights of the holiday. On the eve of Christmas, it is traditional for all family members to gather and share a special

▲ A Christmas tree lights up Moscow's Red Square for New Year's. New Year's is the biggest holiday of the year in Russia and is followed by Orthodox Christmas on January 7.

meal. The various foods and customs surrounding this meal differ in Russia from village to village and from family to family, but certain aspects remain the same. The **fast** is typically broken after the evening worship service or once the first star appears. The dinner that follows is very much a celebration, although meat is still not permitted.

Kutya (or *kutia*), a type of porridge, is the dish served to break the fast. The ingredients have symbolic meanings; the grains represent immortality, and the honey and poppy seeds symbolize happiness, success, and peace. The family eats it from a common dish to express unity. Some families throw a spoonful of the *kutya* at the ceiling. If it sticks, the **superstition** is that there will be a good honey harvest that year. Often a house blessing is offered at this time.

Once the first star has appeared in the sky, the real feasting begins. Although all of the food served is strictly lenten (suitable for Lent; spare and meatless), it is served in an unusually festive and anticipatory manner and style. The Russians call this meal the "Holy Supper." The family gathers around the table to honor the coming Christ child. A white tablecloth, symbolic of Christ's swaddling clothes, covers the table. Hay is brought forth as a reminder of the poverty of the place where Jesus was born. A tall white candle is placed in the center of the table, symbolic of Christ, "the Light of the World." A large round loaf of Lenten bread, *pagach*–symbolic of Christ, the Bread of Life–is placed next to the candle. Traditionally 12 foods were served to represent the 12 apostles, or followers, of Christ.

The meal begins with the Lord's Prayer, traditionally led by the father of the family. A prayer of thanksgiving for all the blessings of the past year is said and then prayers for the good things in the coming year are offered. The head of the family greets those present with the traditional Christmas greeting: "Christ is Born!" The family members respond: "Glorify Him!"

The Mother of the family blesses each person present with honey in the form of a cross on each forehead, saying: "In the Name of the Father, and of the Son, and of the Holy Spirit, may you have sweetness and many good things in life and in the new year."

Following this, everyone partakes of the bread, dipping it first in honey and then in chopped garlic. Honey is symbolic of the sweetness of life, and garlic of the bitterness. The family then enjoys their "Holy Supper." After dinner, no dishes are washed. This is when the family opens small gifts. Then they go to midnight services. Near the end of the service, everyone walks outside carrying sources of light such as candles, torches, and homemade lanterns. They parade around the church, led by the highest-ranking church member. This ceremony is called Krestny Khod. Once the parishioners have circled the church, they go back inside for more carols and hymns. They finally arrive home between 2 and 3 A.M.

Christmas is followed by a period known as Christmastide (Svyatki). During this 12-day period, both pagan and Christian elements are clearly visible.

In Russia in the past, groups of people masqueraded as manger animals and went from house to house, having a rousing good time and singing songs known as *kolyadki*. Some *kolyadki* were a blend of pastoral carols to the baby Jesus and songs to the ancient solar goddess Kolyada. She was thought to bring the lengthening days of sunlight through the winter. In return for their songs, the singers were offered food and coins, which they gladly accepted before moving on to the next house. In other locations, the custom was to dirty one's face with coal dusk, and dress like the opposite sex. The young people then gathered as a crowd and went from house to house singing. After the seriousness of the days leading up to Christmas, this was a time to relax and have fun so that everyone could endure the long northern winter. Not everyone follows these customs today, but it is still common to hold lots of noisy outdoor festivals. Celebrants may ride in a troika (sledge drawn by three horses) and participate in presentations of traditional stories. A carnival-like atmosphere prevails.

Christmastide foods include bliny (Russian pancakes), caviar (fish eggs), pies, and honey. Christmastide consists of 12 days–the 12 days of Christmas–ending on January 19th with the Christening (also known as Theophany). The Christening commemorates Christ's baptism in the Jordan River by St. John the Baptist. Religious processions take place all over Russia as priests and believers go to rivers, lakes, springs, or any other nearby bodies of water. With prayers and chants, the priests submerge a cross into the ice-covered water, thereby blessing it. The blessed water can

CHRISTMASTIDE TRADITIONS IN RUSSIA

Fortune-telling is popular during Christmastide; girls melt wax and pour it into cold water or snow. The resulting shape is then held up in front of a piece of white paper and the shadows are supposed to reveal future events, especially concerning admirers to come. This method is still popular. Another old superstition consisted of a girl kicking off her shoe. The direction the shoe pointed after it fell indicated from where her bridegroom would arrive. Or if a man picked up the shoe, the girl would marry a man with that name. During the old days, there were marriage "fairs," where prospective couples could meet. Many girls still believe that Christmastide is a good time to keep one's eye out for a husband.

▲ A Bulgarian man proudly displays the cross he recovered from the ice-cold waters of a lake during a Theophany ritual held each year on January 6. According to Bulgarian custom, the man who recovers the cross on Epiphany day will enjoy good health all year.

then be used to consecrate the houses of the faithful. Anyone who wishes to be baptized at this time can also be christened with the ice water.

■ Hanukkah in Russia

By the early 21st century, Hanukkah was celebrated across the former Soviet Union. Why is this important? The answer requires one to look back in time. The religious persecution of the Jews in the former Soviet Union reached new levels of violence and cruelty during the 75 years of communist rule. Those Jews who stood up for their beliefs were often arrested, tortured, sent to slave labor camps, or executed. By the end of the 20th century, Jews living in Russia had—for a long time—been deprived of their national, cultural, and spiritual rights.

Watch footage of Hanukkah celebrations in central Moscow.

Despite the religious persecution, the emigration of Soviet Jews to other countries, and the absence of freedom of worship during the communist regimes, there still remains a Jewish presence in Moscow as well as other parts of Russia. With the collapse of the Soviet system in the 1980s and 1990s, the third-largest Jewish population in the world was given an opportunity to worship without fear for the first time in most of their lives. Rabbis traveled to Russia from various countries in order to help educate Russian Jews about their faith. In Moscow, the first Jewish Community Center was opened in late 2000.

Not long after, the first public candle lighting ceremony in Moscow took place. The mayor had the honor of lighting the *shamash*. Afterward, there were fireworks, and a men's choir sang while people danced. The rabbi who lit the candle for the first night spoke about the miracle of Hanukkah: "The miracle of Hanukkah is what God did for us . . . today the possibility to openly celebrate Jewish holidays and light a menorah on a central square in Moscow represents another present-day miracle."

■ Christmas in the United Kingdom and Ireland

The United Kingdom includes England, Scotland, Wales, and the province of Northern Ireland. The United Kingdom and the independent country of Ireland have large Christian populations, and so for them Christmas is an important religious as well as secular holiday. Christmas is celebrated there beginning on December 24 and it lasts until Boxing Day, December 26.

Boxing Day, also known as Saint Stephen's Day, is important to people in the United Kingdom because Saint Stephen was the first Christian martyr. In early times, many people had to work on Christmas. The servants in the great houses and castles of the day then got the next day off to visit with friends and family. For many servants, their employers would place clothing, food, money, and other gifts into boxes for them. The servants would receive these gifts as they were leaving for the day. Another reason this is called Boxing Day is because of the money collected in church boxes for charity. This is the traditional date when charity boxes were opened and the money distributed to the needy.

Many people have sung about Boxing Day for years without realizing it. The song "Good King Wenceslas" originated with the feast of Saint Stephen. A man named Wenceslas became king of Bohemia (now the Czech Republic) in the year 922. The Christmas carol tells of his generosity and kindness. The king, accompanied by his page, carried a meal of mince pie and logs to a peasant on Saint Stephen's Day. It was very cold and the page became scared in the dark. Wenceslas told the page to step into his own footprints for safety. The page did so. His footing became steady and his feet were warmed. The carol is unusual because no mention is made of the nativity.

Although Boxing Day originated in England as a time for the employers to show their appreciation to workers, it is generally embraced today as an additional day of relaxation following Christmas Day.

The 26th is also a time of great fun and gaiety in Ireland and Wales, where from ancient times the local people have celebrated the Day of the Wren. Traditions involve boys and girls, young and old, visiting neighbors' houses while dressed in colorful costumes to collect donations for charities. Welsh holiday celebrations feature nights organized around the activity of making (and eating) toffee. A tradition unique to the United Kingdom and its territories is the broadcast of the Queen's Christmas speech. The tradition began in 1932 with George V. Queen Elizabeth II has chosen to continue the tradition. Her topic varies from year to year, but she usually talks about issues that are of significance at the time. With satellite radio, the Internet, and television, listeners all around the globe can tune in to hear her address. Except for the Queen's speech and the celebration of Boxing Day, most Christmas festivities are very similar in the United Kingdom and United States, because of the number of English-speaking colonists who came from the United Kingdom. Christmas cards were first produced in England, and the British also introduced eggnog, as well as traditional desserts such as mince pie.

The American version of the Yule log also came straight from traditions in the United Kingdom, especially England. In the English tradition, the biggest log available was cut down so that it would burn during the entire 12 days of Christmas. There were other superstitions or customs families followed in order to have good luck. For example, a scrap from the previous year's log was used to light the new log. During the year, the scrap was kept under the bed of the homeowner, which was supposed to keep the house safe from lightning or fire.

Roast turkey is part of a **longstanding** English tradition of the Christmas dinner. Most British families continue to eat dishes similar to those served in the United States for Christmas. They also serve others that have never become popular in the United States, such as bread sauce and Christmas plum pudding called *furmenty*.

The English also pull "crackers" during Christmas. Christmas crackers are party favors made of cardboard tubes wrapped in foil and bright paper. They are wrapped to look like a giant piece of candy. A person on each side takes hold of one end and they pull at the same time. The cracker pops like a cap gun. Inside there is usually a small toy or a silly hat.

Mummering is another Christmas custom in the United Kingdom. People called mummers put on colorful clothes and masks and perform plays usually based on Bible stories. Mummering is most common in England, where the people of a town will gather together to watch the mummer processions and plays. Philadelphia in the United States has its own version of the mummer's parade, but the city includes it as part of their New Year's celebration.

IRELAND AND WALES

December 26 is known as *La Fheile Stiofan*, or the Day of the Wren, in Ireland and Wales. In ancient times, the wren was considered a special type of bird. It was often used as a sacrifice to the gods. In later times, the wren became a symbol of treachery.

It was the custom on the Day of the Wren, which is pronounced "wran," for groups of boys to go singing and dancing from house to house. Usually accompanied by musicians, these boys wore colorful costumes and straw hats. Each group had its own leader, who would carry a dead wren. These groups became known as Straw Boys, Mummers, or Wren Boys, depending on the location. Gradually, the real dead bird has been replaced by a fake one, and girls and adults often join in the visits at various houses. Money that is collected is usually donated to a school or charity.

Ireland is also home to another Christmas custom called the "laden table." After dinner, the table is set again, this time with bread containing caraway seeds and raisins, a pitcher of milk, and a lit candle. The door is left unlatched, so that any hungry wanderer—including Mary and Joseph—can find food within. In many Irish homes, the youngest child is given the honor of lighting a candle to place in the window. This light is a beckoning reminder of the difficulties Mary and Joseph had of finding a place to stay. Today, an electric light may take the place of the candle for reasons of safety.

▲ A four-year-old girl tells Santa what she wants for Christmas.

EUROPEAN TRADITIONS AND CUSTOMS ■ 65

In Wales caroling is called *eisteddfodde*. (*Eisteddfodd* refers to a Welsh gathering to share music, poetry, and literature. A National Eisteddfod is held annually in August.) Sometimes the carolers are accompanied by a harp. Village choirs often compete against each other to see who is best at performing the same carol.

In rural areas, the main Christmas service used to be called *plygain*, which apparently means "before cock-crow." It lasted from 4 A.M. until the sun rose on Christmas Day. Carols were a central aspect of the service—sung by individuals, choirs, trios, and quartets. The custom was discontinued in the 19th century, but recently Methodist chapels have revived it, especially in middle Wales.

Noson Gyflaith (the Toffee Evening) was also a popular Welsh custom. Visitors would be invited for Christmas Eve dinner, after which everyone would play games, tell stories, and pull toffee. Once the hot sugar syrup reached the right temperature, it was poured out on a hard surface that had been buttered so the toffee would not stick to it. Participants would grease their fingers and gingerly begin the process of repeatedly pulling the strands apart, then gathering the sticky mass back into a clump. It was easier (and more fun) to work in pairs. Gradually, the toffee became pale and brittle, which meant enough air had been worked into the mass, and it had cooled enough to be cracked into pieces. Supposedly the toffee curled as it cooled and formed the initials of one's true love. In Wales, toffee is also called "taffi," "ffani," "cyflaith," or "Butterwelsh." The toffee is made from sugar syrup and butter, flavored with extra ingredients such as peppermint extract, molasses, lemon, or orange. Welsh toffee is probably more like American taffy, whereas in Ireland and England, cooks add cream and more butter, resulting in a richer flavor. The purpose of the toffee evening was supposedly to help people stay awake long enough for *plygain* at 4 A.M.

SCOTLAND DISAPPROVES OF CHRISTMAS

In the 1500s many people in Scotland were part of a movement to reform the Catholic Church called the Protestant Reformation. By 1583 any bakers who made special Yule breads could be fined. (However, their fines would be lessened if they gave out the names of their celebrating customers.) In 1638, the General Assembly in Edinburgh, Scotland's capital, tried to abolish the celebration of Yuletide completely. Christmas became three solemn days of prayer, fasting, and church services. Even after the English started easing their anti-Christmas policies, the Scots continued to follow their own ways. Christmas was made a working day to keep people from having time to celebrate. Scottish New Year's—known as Hogmanay—gradually became a bigger and bigger celebration. It was as if the energy and fun of Christmas got rerouted to a different day. Today, Hogmanay in Scotland is like one big street party, including dancing, feasting, partying, and specific customs involving bonfires and parades that recall pagan customs.

TEXT-DEPENDENT QUESTIONS

1: Where do Sephardic Jews originally hail from?

2: Who wrote the lyrics to the Christmas carol "Silent Night"?

3: What is the name for the Scottish New Year?

RESEARCH PROJECTS

1: Research the figure of Befana, a character out of Italian folklore who delivers gifts to children on Epiphany eve. Write a brief report including the history of the legend, facts about Befana's appearance, and how the tradition lives on in Italy today.

2: Research more about the Jewish holiday of Purim, including its history, when it takes place, and associated customs and traditions. Write a brief report summarizing your findings.

Latin American and Caribbean Traditions and Customs

In Latin America, Christianity came at the point of a sword: the sword of Spanish conquistadores, or conquerors, who were searching for gold. Sent by the king and queen of Spain 500 years ago, the conquistadores forced their religion on the native people they encountered. Today Catholicism is the predominant religion of Latin America, and most of its people are descended from both **indigenous** people and Spaniards.

La Navidad, or the birth of Jesus, is celebrated in a lively way in Latin America. Lights and ornaments of all colors are used to decorate Christmas trees in people's homes, though decorating the outside of the house is not a common practice. On the top of the tree a figure representing Father Christmas is carefully attached to the highest branch. In many homes, one can find a nativity scene, representing the birth of Jesus. This is

WORDS TO UNDERSTAND

Gourd: A fruit with a hard rind produced by certain plants.
Indigenous: A person, plant, or other entity native to a given area.
Kosher: Food that adheres to certain Jewish dietary laws.

◀ Ecuadorian soldiers wear historic uniforms as they march in the annual Pase del Niño (Christmas Eve) parade.

called the *pesebre* (crib) or *nacimiento* (birth), or occasionally a *retablo* (altarpiece). The *pesebre* manger scene has a place of honor, and stays up until New Year's. The *pesebre* often is a reflection of the culture of the country. For example, in Bolivia, some families put their nativity scene inside a **gourd** that has been hollowed out, dried, and then painted in bright colors. In Ecuador, the figures wear Ecuadorian costumes or local dress. In Colombia, the *pesebre* can end up being as large as a model train layout, with families having good-natured competitions to see who can build the most elaborate one.

On December 24, many families open the presents under their Christmas trees, although in certain countries, such as Uruguay and Mexico, presents are brought by the Three Kings, who don't arrive until January 6. The influence of the United States continues to affect customs in Latin America, which may explain why in many places, gift-opening has been moved to December 25.

December in Latin America varies greatly in terms of climate, depending on how close one is to the equator, or whether the celebration is taking place in the mountains or at lower elevations.

▲ A giant illuminated ship is suspended above the Medellin River as part of the annual Christmas lights show in Medellin, Colombia.

▲ Many parks in the capital city of Bogota in Colombia are decorated with lights for the Christmas season.

Those who live where December is warm often hold their holiday parties outside. They may cook outside or have picnics.

Regardless of climate, Christians in Latin America usually go to church on Christmas Eve and then go home to celebrate the holiday with their families. In the evening, many adults go out dancing. They drink champagne at midnight and watch the firework displays that are common in the region at that time. If they have not done so already, families open their presents on Christmas morning.

Jews were present in South America at least as early as the 17th century (this is known because when Catholic Brazil forced them to leave, they became the first Jews of North America, taking refuge in the religiously tolerant settlement of New Amsterdam in modern New York City). As it happens, the Jewish population centers in Latin America of the early 21st century developed primarily after the Holocaust, through the emigration of European Jews to existing small communities in urban locations such as Buenos Aires, Argentina, and Caracas, Venezuela. In metropolitan areas with large populations such as these, Hanukkah is often celebrated with public gatherings. Menorah lightings, indoor and outdoor meals, and even walking city tours are all done in groups as a way to mark the holiday.

■ A Vibrant Jewish Community in Argentina

For the Argentineans, Hanukkah is more informal than in places such as the United States. Many Jews enjoy the holiday's relaxed atmosphere and its emphasis on family and socializing, and the weather cooperates as Hanukkah falls in the middle of summer in Argentina.

Because so many of Argentina's Jews come from different countries, there are numerous variations on how to celebrate. Giving Hanukkah *gelt* and small gifts is common, but not on the scale that North American Jews participate in.

According to some estimates, there are more than 230,000 Jews in Argentina. This gives Argentina the largest Jewish population in Latin America. About 180,000 of Argentina's Jews reside in the metropolitan area of Buenos Aires. The rest of the Jewish population lives in cities and small towns throughout the country. There are many temples in Buenos Aires, and during Hanukkah, Jews can attend public menorah lightings in several different locations, including a state-sponsored ceremony in Plaza San Martin. Many people live in apartment buildings, so menorahs shine from windows that are

A KOSHER MCDONALD'S IN BUENOS AIRES

The neighborhood of Once in Buenos Aires is mostly Jewish, and is similar in size to the Lower East Side of New York City. Once is home to the only **kosher** McDonald's outside of Israel. The menu is typical of McDonald's restaurants everywhere, but there is no form of dairy available, since dairy and meat are not served together in a kosher setting.

closely grouped together, which makes for a beautiful display.

Many people fly into Buenos Aires to join in the Hanukkah festivities. In the Plaza Uruguay large crowds gather to watch the lighting of the largest menorah in South America as they listen to klezmer music. Klezmer music is deliberately meant to sound like the cries, wails, and laughter of a human voice. Though klezmer musicians do not limit themselves to religious music, the expressive style is modeled after Jewish cantors, singers who are chosen to lead prayers and sing in synagogues. Klezmer bands often play during joyful holiday celebrations such as Hanukkah.

People also enjoy kosher *chorizo* (a pepperoni-like sausage) during Hanukkah. There are lively celebrations and special dinners held to bring together Jews from all parts of the world on these special nights.

KLEZMER MUSIC

Klezmer music originated with Ashkenazi and Hasidic Jews, and in the beginning *klezmer* referred solely to performances on musical instruments. Gradually, klezmer music came to include the musicians themselves. The music began as dance music, frequently played at weddings and other gatherings, but continues to evolve. Lyrics, song titles, and the musical terms are usually in Yiddish, the German dialect that includes words from Hebrew as well as some modern languages. The instruments used in klezmer music usually include the violin, cymbalom (a stringed instrument similar to a dulcimer), clarinet, accordion, trombone, trumpet, piano, and poyk (a frame drum).

■ Santa Claus Wears Silk in Brazil

Brazil occupies about half of South America, and is the only country in the continent where the principal language is Portuguese, not Spanish. At Christmas, the nativity scene is called a *presépio* instead of *pesebre*. What is known as the Misa de gallo (Rooster's Mass) in Spanish-speaking countries, in Brazil is called the Missa do galo. Both are referred to as such because the rooster would have been the first animal to announce Jesus' birth. Typically, the Missa do galo is a midnight mass that ends around 1 A.M.

In northern Brazil, the Christmas pageants feature shepherdesses instead of shepherds, and the animals can talk, though they have fewer lines than the human characters. There is also a scene in which gypsies kidnap the baby Jesus and the three kings have to get him back.

Since it is hot in December in Brazil, Santa Claus, who is called Papai Noel, dresses in silk or other light fabric. He may even arrive on a surfboard or by helicopter, having come, as Brazilian children believe, from Greenland. Since in Brazil there aren't a lot of chimneys for Santa Claus to come down, Papai Noel puts presents in shoes the children have left out. Sometimes he hides them in other places around the house, such as under a bed.

The big Christmas dinner for Brazilians takes place at noon or during the evening of December 25. Turkey and a dish called "chester" are the most common foods. Chester is a mixture of turkey and chicken. Dessert consists of *rabanadas*, or Portuguese fried toast. The dessert originated in Portugal and is made from French bread, eggs, and cinnamon sugar.

¡Feliz Navidad! in Mexico City

In July 2008, the estimated population of Mexico was 109,955,400. This is an impressive population in a country that is slightly less than three times the size of the state of Texas. Of these approximately 84 million, or 76.5 percent, considered themselves Roman Catholic, and another 6.3 percent Protestant. This translates to more than 90 million Christians in Mexico. Therefore, more than 90 million Mexicans celebrate Christmas as a religious holiday, while others celebrate it as

▲ Every year for the last 400 years, residents of this Mexico City neighborhood have celebrated nine Posadas (*Posada* in Spanish means *lodging* or *shelter*) and taken their sacred Ninopan, or Baby Jesus of the Place, in a procession to the church for a mass. The Posada party is celebrated each day from December 16 to 24. These celebrations commemorate Mary and Joseph's journey from Nazareth to Bethlehem in search of shelter.

a secular holiday. The culture of Mexico is made up of a colorful blend of peoples and traditions. There are pre-Hispanic, native civilizations, and Hispanic cultures. There are also influences from France, Germany, the United States, Africa, and Asia visible in the culture of Mexico.

Mexicans take part in a nine-day ritual called Posadas, which is also celebrated (with variations) in Colombia, Honduras, Nicaragua, Guatemala, El Salvador, and Belize. The ritual's purpose is to remind people of the difficulties that Mary and Joseph had in trying to find a place to stay in Bethlehem. Posadas means the same as the English word "inns." December 16 is when the tradition begins and it does not end until Noche Buena, "Holy Night," which is Christmas Eve.

During Posadas, both children and adults usually walk together as pilgrims. These *peregrinos* (pilgrims) travel from house to house, singing a song that asks for lodging for Mary and Joseph.

En el nombre del Cielo
os pido posada,
pues no puede andar
mi esposa amada.

[In the name of Heaven
I ask you for lodging,
because she cannot walk,
my beloved wife.]

Often pilgrims will carry lit candles and statues of Mary and Joseph. It is common for whoever leads the procession to hold a *farolito*, which is a candle with a little lampshade. Sometimes a girl dresses as Mary, and a boy as Joseph to take part in some very traditional Posadas. When the pilgrims ask for shelter, the owners at the first two houses refuse. This is done in a song.

Aquí no es mesón;
sigan adelante.
Yo no puedo abrir,
no sea algún tunante.

[This is no inn,
keep going.
I cannot open up,
in case you are a rascal.]

Then when the pilgrims reach the house where the hosts will hold the party, the owners pretend they are innkeepers. This time they let the pilgrims come in. The owners sing:

*Entren, Santos Peregrinos,
reciban este rincón
no de esta pobre morada
sino de corazón.*

[Enter, Holy Pilgrims,
accept this small corner;
not of this humble dwelling,
but of my heart.]

Every night a different family in the neighborhood acts as the innkeeper. The guests sometimes join together to pray the Rosary, a traditional Catholic set of prayers. They often sing Christmas carols, or *villancicos*. Then a piñata is broken. A piñata is usually an animal or star-shaped papier-mâché vessel that is filled with treats such as fruit, sugar cane, or nuts. One person is blindfolded and then given a stick. The piñata is suspended above the crowd, within reach of the stick, but higher than the heads of the people below. Someone gives the piñata a push, and it begins to swing around while the blindfolded person tries to hit it with the stick. The piñata often swings in different directions once it is hit, so the challenge is not only to sense its location and hit it again, but also to hit it hard enough so it breaks open. Participants sing special songs while people take turns being the one blindfolded. The following song dates all the way back to the year 1557.

ORIGINS OF PIÑATAS

The custom of breaking a piñata is centuries old, and it probably began in China. The explorer Marco Polo mentioned in his writings that Mandarins (Chinese) used items best described as piñatas to celebrate the beginning of spring. The Mandarins would hit hollow figures that were filled with seeds. These figures were made in animal shapes. Afterward the people gathered the pieces of the piñatas and used them to build a large fire. Then each person would take home some of the ashes. They believed that the ashes would bring them good luck in the coming year.

▲ An assortment of piñatas in a market in Mexico City, Mexico. Traditionally, piñatas are broken open by children before Christmas to get at the candy, nuts, and fruit inside.

▲ Mexico is not the only place where piñatas play a part in Christmas celebrations. Here children in a town in Honduras celebrate the holiday by breaking the piñata.

No quiero níquel ni quiero plata:
yo lo que quiero es romper la piñata.

[I don't want nickel, I don't want silver:
What I want is to break the piñata.]

Spanish missionaries who came to North America in the 16th century brought with them the tradition of a piñata. Today the piñata no longer has any religious meaning. In Mexico, one sees piñatas hanging in the streets, especially during the Christmas season. In addition to piñatas being broken at the parties of Posadas, it is common for piñatas to be used as part of birthday celebrations. This custom is seen not only in Mexico, but also in the United States and other parts of the world where it has been enthusiastically embraced. Besides piñatas made in the forms of stars or animals, piñatas that look like characters from popular culture are now available.

A quick and easy recipe for Mexican Christmas fruit punch.

In Mexico during Posadas, once the people have broken the piñatas, there are a number of traditional foods to enjoy. These include such dishes as *buñuelos* (sugar-covered fried pastries), *colación* (candies), tamales (cornmeal dough that is stuffed with fillings, wrapped up in corn leaves, and steamed until the dough holds together), and *ponche*, a type of punch. The *ponche* is usually flavored with such seasonal fruits as *tejocotes* (much like crabapples), oranges, guavas, plums, and prunes. Vanilla and cinnamon are often included. Recipes vary regionally.

On Noche Buena, the whole family goes to mass together. After that, they all eat dinner with other family members and any friend who does not have family nearby.

 **TEXT-DEPENDENT QUESTIONS**

1: Where does the state-sponsored Hanukkah ceremony take place in Buenos Aires?

2: What is Santa Claus called in Brazil?

3: What is Posadas, and where is it celebrated?

▲ A traditional tamale, shown here, is made of meat, chili, and *masa* (cornmeal) wrapped in corn husks and steamed. The tradition of holiday tamales traces its roots back to the Aztecs in Mexico, who ate tamales for sacred occasions.

 **RESEARCH PROJECTS**

1: Find a famous klezmer musician from any era. Research his or her biography, including the instrument(s) played, songs written and/or performed, and influence on the klezmer tradition. Write a brief biographical sketch summarizing your findings.

2: Research Christmas customs and traditions in a Latin American country not covered in this chapter, such as Chile. Write a brief report comparing and contrasting this country's Christmas traditions with those of other Latin American nations.

Middle Eastern Traditions and Customs

As a region, the Middle East is partially a political construction of the 19th century though it has always been a distinct crossroads of cultures. It is in its heart–Israel, the tiny nation on the eastern edge of the Mediterranean Sea–that both the historical Christmas story and the events commemorated in Hanukkah celebrations occurred. Situated between Egypt and Lebanon, Israel is just slightly smaller than the state of New Jersey. The official language of Israel is Hebrew, but Arabic is the official language for the minority group of Arabs. The most common foreign language heard in Israel is English.

WORDS TO UNDERSTAND

Disengagement: The process of withdrawing from a place, situation, or activity.

Embroidery: The art of decorating cloth with patterns of stitched thread and other materials.

Vestments: Ceremonial robes worn by priests and other clergy during religious services.

◀ The Bahai gardens decorated for the holidays, in Haifa, Israel.

The major religions of Judaism, Christianity, and Islam all began in the Middle East, and share some common roots in the region's history. The Hanukkah story of the rededication of the Temple is significant not just because a temple was rededicated, but because it was a temple located in the holiest city in Judaism. Jerusalem, the city of biblical King David, is one of the oldest cities in the world and has been the focus of Jewish spirituality for centuries.

About 6 miles from Jerusalem lies Bethlehem, the place Christians believe Jesus was born. Reminders of the location show up in Christmas pageants, nativity scenes, religious services, and carols such as "Oh Little Town of Bethlehem," and "O Come, O Come Emmanuel." As a global magnet for people who live in very different cultures and climates, the mystery and wonder surrounding Jesus' birth is intensified by what seems to them an exotic location, complete with camels, kings, and deserts under starry skies.

WHERE THE SHEPHERDS KEPT WATCH

The Shepherds' Fields lie just outside of Bethlehem. This area is where the shepherds are believed to have been approached by an angel who told them of Jesus' birth. Three "rival" sites lie not far from each other. One is the site the Greek Orthodox church identifies as historically accurate and the other is the site that Roman Catholics believe is correct. Both sites have been excavated and there have been churches and monasteries there since at least the fourth century. Protestants claim still a third site at the YMCA of Beit Sahour as the place where the angel appeared to the shepherds and told them of Jesus' birth.

■ Christmas in Israel

Since there are many Christian denominations—or groups with different beliefs about how to practice Christianity—Christmas in Bethlehem is a major event. Each group gets an opportunity to hold services and have processions through the streets. The groups that celebrate Christmas in Bethlehem include Catholic, Protestant, Greek Orthodox, Ethiopian, Armenian, and more. Since different groups celebrate Christmas on different days, the celebrations stretch out over several weeks. Many of the essential traditions of other countries, such as Christmas trees, gift giving, and the journey of Santa Claus are retained by these Israeli immigrant communities.

The Roman Catholics and Protestants celebrate on December 25; Greek, Syrian, and other Orthodox Christians observe Christmas on January 7; and the Armenian Christians do so on January 18. Some hold services in their local churches, whereas others organize trips to the Shepherds' Fields or the Church of the Nativity. Most processions pass through Manger Square, which is the plaza outside the Church of the Nativity, located on the traditional site of Jesus' birth.

The holy **vestments**, or ceremonial robes worn by the various priests and other clergy of the churches are often elaborate, covered with symbolic colors and ornate **embroidery**. Many of the church leaders wear very distinctive headgear, too. The result is that processions are every bit as colorful and exotic as any visitor could imagine.

EXTRAORDINARY HOLIDAY FEATS

Many people try to set records related to Hanukkah. For example, in 1997, a group created a large menorah near the Jerusalem-Tel Aviv highway. This menorah was completely made from metal pipe. It was greater than 60 feet tall and it weighed more than 17 metric tons. It covered 600 square meters of ground. Each of the eight nights of Hanukkah, a crane was used to lift a rabbi up to light the candles.

■ Hanukkah in Israel

Jews have been in the Middle East for thousands of years. The settlement of modern Israel as a Jewish homeland goes back to the end of World War II in 1945 and British **disengagement** from the region. Israel, or the State of Israel, is overwhelmingly Jewish. There are about 6,500,000 people living there. Of these, more than 75 percent are Jewish. Not all Jews living in Israel observe all of the traditions and rituals of the religion, but Hanukkah is a happy and festive time for most Jews in Israel. Unlike other solemn holidays with long, formal services, Hanukkah takes place primarily in the home. Because the holiday skews more toward being historical than purely spiritual, it has traditionally not been seen as a holiday of major importance in the Jewish faith, although it has served over the years as a bright reminder of victory over persecution. Not so much a holiday of inner reflection, it is a time of outward joy and the giving of little gifts—such as the chocolate discs called *gelt* that are wrapped in gold foil to look like ancient coins. *Gelt* is often wagered in games of dreidel played by Jewish children after the Hanukkah lights have been kindled. Due to the tradition of gift giving, the holiday has a commercial aspect as well. Stores feature special displays and offer Hanukkah gifts such as chocolates or crystal in symbolic shapes.

▲ An Israeli boy, celebrating the Jewish festival of Hanukkah, lights the menorah candles.

◀ The Israeli president lights the Hanukkah candles at his home in Jerusalem. Although Hanukkah is not a major holiday in Judaism, it is enjoyed by young and old alike.

In Israel, as in all parts of the world, Hanukkah begins on the 25th day of Kislev, which usually places it in December. The central ceremony of the holiday is the lighting of the menorah candles on each of the eight nights. In Israel, it is not surprising that Hanukkah focuses largely on the theme of the Jews restoring their right to self-government. Children have a holiday from school throughout Hanukkah, but businesses remain open. Blessings are recited each night, and prayers of thanks and praise are offered in keeping with the recitation of how God strengthened the ancient Hebrews in their resistance to Greek oppression.

Experience scenes of Hanukkah in Jerusalem.

TEXT-DEPENDENT QUESTIONS

1: What is the official language of Israel?

2: On what date do Orthodox Christians celebrate Christmas?

3: What is the name for the chocolate discs consumed during Hanukkah?

RESEARCH PROJECTS

1: Research the Christmas traditions of the Coptic Christians of Egypt, including their fasting practices before the feast, customary foods of Christmas day, and any special prayer and devotional practices. Write a brief report summarizing your findings.

2: Research the history of Judaism in Morocco, with a special focus on Hanukkah traditions. Write a brief report touching on the changes in Jewish population in Morocco over the years, the languages spoken, and any unique customs of Moroccan Jews.

MIDDLE EASTERN TRADITIONS AND CUSTOMS ■ 85

North American Traditions and Customs

There is a tendency to think of Christmas in North America as a unified package of traditions that has been handed down from generation to generation. In fact, it is a mishmash of cultural customs borrowed from the various groups of people who have come to North America over time, sometimes mingled with the traditions of the Native Americans who were here already. Even today Christmas celebrations still hold onto the distinct flavor of the people who brought their customs with them when they first settled. For example, in French Canada, Père Noël is the name of the gift bringer known as Santa Claus elsewhere. In Louisiana, every year people light hundreds of

> **WORDS TO UNDERSTAND**
> **Garland**: A wreath of leaves and/or flowers.
> **Merriment**: Festivity, fun, gaiety.
> **Unrest**: A state of agitation or disruption.

◀ All across the U.S., Christmas trees are common sights during the holiday season. This tree stands tall, decked out in red, white, and blue in San Antonio, Texas.

bonfires along the Mississippi to guide Papa Noël south. A Cajun version of the Santa Claus story has Papa Noël arriving on a pierogue (a flat-bottomed boat common to the bayou), drawn by alligators. The Mexican tradition of *luminarias* or *farolitos* (little lights) lives on in the thousands of radiant paper-bag lanterns that adorn New Mexican cities such as Santa Fe and Albuquerque at Christmastime.

North America encompasses not just a variety landscapes and peoples but religions and philosophies too. In addition to Christmas, Hanukkah and pagan solstice celebrations are observed across the region at this time of year. Because North America has a proud tradition and legal culture of tolerating diversity in religion, it is a special place for Jews and has been for centuries. This acceptance and curiosity extends to indigenous practices and beliefs. For many Americans with no Native American blood at all, the rituals and understandings of the native peoples add meaning to their lives.

▲ A man cuts down the family's Christmas tree at a Christmas tree farm in North Carolina.

For Christians, Christmas is the celebration of Jesus' birth, which they may commemorate by going to church, putting up a nativity scene, and singing hymns and carols about the birth of Christ. For many young children, the greatest excitement of Christmas comes from their belief in a jolly, bearded, fat man dressed in a red suit who delivers presents to well-behaved children. Most of the year he lives at the North Pole with a wife who looks like his twin. His helpers are tiny, clever people who mostly dress in green and wear pointed hats. Their shoes too curl up at the tips.

For weeks before December 25, the children eagerly anticipate the arrival of the plump, bearded figure known as Santa Claus. Finally, on Christmas Eve he loads a gigantic bag stuffed full of toys into his sleigh, which is hitched to a group of 13 reindeer, including one in front who has a nose like a red light bulb. He and the reindeer then launch into the air, flying high above a moonlit landscape. He stops at every house, slides down each chimney, delivers all the gifts, and makes it home before the sun comes up. Family members wake to find stockings dangling from the mantelpiece, bulging with the shapes of the mysterious contents inside. In a place of honor, a tree, real or artificial, sparkles with lights, ornaments, tinsel, and candy canes. Below it, brightly wrapped presents gleaming with ribbon lie scattered in tempting heaps. For Christians and non-Christians Christmas is a time for exchanging gifts, eating foods they rarely eat at any other time of year, listening to Christmas music, and spending time with friends and family.

NATIVE AMERICAN CHRISTMAS

The Native Americans of the United States have their own variations on Christmas traditions that blend pre-Christian practices with newer, more Americanized ones. For instance, those tribes that are able to obtain Christmas trees decorate them with corn, shells, and other natural objects. Instead of electric lights they use mirrors to deflect evil spirits. Other tribes, such as the Hopi of the southwest, fashion nativity scenes from wool, clay, and wood, using animals such as buffalo in place of sheep around the manger. The Native American equivalent of Santa Claus is a figure known as "the Handsome Man." He is a tall brave who dresses completely in white buckskin. On Christmas Eve he makes his rounds, giving gifts to families.

■ First Nations Winter Solstice in Canada

Drive walruses towards me–You Food Dish there below the ice! Send me gifts!

–Old Inuit song

The Native Americans of Canada are known as the aboriginal peoples of Canada, or First Nations. There are three main groups recognized in Canada's Constitution Act of 1982: the Métis, North American Indians, and the Inuit. It is estimated that by 2017 they will represent 4.1 percent of the Canadian population. The original Inuit religion was one of shamanism combined with belief that natural aspects of the world are alive. (Shamans are the spiritual and natural healers of pre-industrial societies.)

Living in the fierce cold of the arctic region, and surviving mostly through fishing and hunting, like many native populations, the indigenous people of Canada have developed extensive knowledge of the natural world through careful observation. They have also made ingenious use of the materials within their environment. People such as the Inuit have also evolved their own myths and stories to explain natural phenomena. For example, when they see the dancing colors of the northern lights, their explanation is that the lights are caused by the souls of people who no longer live on earth. (Western scientists, on the other hand, say that the northern lights are caused by magnetic particles that collide with gas in the atmosphere, making them glow red, green, blue, and violet.)

The Inuits called their winter celebration Quviasugvik, which translates into English as "the time and place of joy." The festival typically took place either late in the fall or in early winter, sometimes at the solstice but essentially to mark the beginning of the hunting season. It lasted for one evening and through the following day. A few records from whalers and other visitors have supplied historians glimpses of how Quviasugvik was celebrated.

During the opening evening, the shamans (*anggakuits*) offered prayers for the community. The Inuit belief was that the spirits of the dead did not go directly to the land of the dead, but stopped and attacked Inuit communities along the way. On this night the community's *anggakuits* would enter a hut to pray for their people's protection from the spirits of the dead and the goddess of the sea, Sedna.

SEDNA–TRAGIC SPIRIT OF THE NEW YEAR

There are several different legends about how Sedna became a goddess. In some versions she is a victim of her father, who chops off her fingers to make her let go of the kayak she is clinging to.

In others she appears to be an evil person who is thrown overboard. In all of the myths, however, there is a scene in which she is tossed into the sea. Her fingers turn into the first seals and marine animals. She becomes a powerful spirit who lives on the floor of the ocean. The Inuit's belief was that in order to have good hunting and a prosperous year, they had to please and respect her, since the game that they hunted was under her command.

On the day of Quviasugvik the whole community participated. Everyone wore protective amulets, or charms, and divided themselves into two groups–the people born in summer (ducks) and those born in winter (ptarmigans, or grouse). They took part in a tug-of war, using a rope made of sealskin. If the ducks won, fine weather was supposed to continue through the winter. If the other side won, the winter would be long and difficult.

Afterward, everyone would gather into a circle. A large container of water was placed in the center, and each person carried a piece of meat. All the participants ate their meat at the same time, while concentrating on good wishes from Sedna. The oldest man dipped a cup into the water, drank, and before passing it to the next person, stated the time and place of his birth. The oldest woman would go next. This action was repeated for each person, even little children, who would be represented by their mothers. Only the children born that year were omitted. Finally, the participants threw gifts to each other with the idea that if they were generous, Sedna would be generous to them. The remainder of the celebration was very informal, involving playing lots of games, feasting on special foods, telling traditional stories, and exchanging community news.

Once the Christian missionaries arrived, Christmas celebrations gradually replaced the traditional winter feasts. The Inuit emphasis on protection from the spirits of the dead was replaced with the Christian emphasis on the return of the light. The missionaries often supplied Western style food and drinks, especially because the Inuit had fewer resources and could not afford to provide for all. The playing of games remained a central feature of the celebration, though sometimes appearing in new forms. In Inuit society, games had a history of being used to dissolve tensions within the community and to transform hostility into friendly competition.

Many dealings between the new Canadian government and the people of the First Nations were much more hostile than those recorded by whalers at the turn of the century, however. When Europeans first arrived in Canada they traded with the indigenous people. They wanted to take home furs, fish, timber, maple syrup, and other products that were abundant in Canada, but not in their countries. As the trappers and hunters were joined by groups of Europeans wishing to acquire land that had traditionally belonged to the First Nations, relations became much more strained. This strain grew worse as the Europeans often dealt dishonestly with them and brought diseases for which the Native Americans had no immunity. In their zeal to spread Christianity, many European missionaries forced their religious beliefs onto the native population.

■ Christmas in Canada

In Canada, Christmas observance is, like Canada itself, more English and more French than observances across its border to the south in the United States. French Canadian children expect a visit from *Père Noël*. They put up crèches, or nativity scenes. Though they are likely to have turkey for their main meal, they also enjoy *boulettes*, or small meatballs. They also consume *tourtière*, a meat pie made from pork, potatoes, and onions, which is served on Christmas Eve.

In Vancouver, as in the coastal states of the United States, Canadians make use of their ships to create colorful Christmas displays and events. For two weeks prior to Christmas, children's choirs board ships to serenade the people from the harbor. The waterfront is decorated with thousands of lights, just as it is elsewhere. In a tradition begun in 1986, traditionally the Christmas lights are lit all across Canada at the same moment: 6:55 P.M. on the first Thursday in December.

Nova Scotia was settled by Scottish Highlanders more than two centuries ago. During the 12 days of Christmas, groups of mummers–in this case known as *belsnicklers*–go from door to door. Similar to trick-or-treaters on Halloween, they wear masks, make rude noises, demand treats, and ring doorbells. While they bring candy or treats for the children of their houses, if they are recognized they are invited in and given refreshments such as lemonade, cider, doughnuts, and cake. *Belsnicklers* also show up in the United States in places such as Maryland or Pennsylvania; anywhere Lutheran or members of the Reformed Church settled. While the custom died out during the Civil War in some locations, it lives on in others.

Like their neighbors in the United States, Canadians use gingerbread houses, Christmas trees, and mistletoe as symbols of the holiday season. For Catholics in Canada, families attend mass before they open gifts and have a Christmas meal together. It is also a custom for these families to visit their Church's crèche after the final services have been held on Christmas Day.

■ Hanukkah in Canada

For Jews in Canada, as well as in the United States, one of the biggest challenges is to hold onto their religious traditions when they are surrounded by a majority that is celebrating Christmas either as a religious holiday or a secular one. Some Jews feel that making Hanukkah a "bigger" holiday is not a reaction to political situations in the world, but a response to the overwhelming

▲ In French Canada, Santa Claus is known as Père Noël. Here a street in old historic Quebec City, Canada, is lit up by Christmas decorations.

emphasis on Christmas. However, some rabbis and other Jewish leaders see the emphasis on Christmas as a perfect opportunity to be reminded of Hanukkah's meaning. When the ancient Jews were surrounded by Greek culture, some of them adopted Greek customs and dress. The Maccabees are remembered because they refused to be absorbed by the dominant culture. They were ordinary people who took a stand against the pressure to change their customs and beliefs.

■ Christmas in the United States

Many of the Christmas customs considered traditional in the United States are actually not very old. For example, when the Pilgrims founded the settlement of Plymouth in Massachusetts, Thanksgiving was more important than Christmas. In fact, the second year after the settlement was founded, the governor banned Christmas completely. This was because in the opinion of the

▲ Men and women dressed as old-fashioned Christmas carolers, sing Christmas carols in Wisconsin.

Pilgrims, not only the Catholic Church of England but even the Protestant church in England–the Church of England–had become corrupt. The Pilgrims did not believe they could reform the Church, so they decided to separate from it. First they tried living in Holland, but found it too difficult. After 12 years they returned to England. From there, 102 of them set out for North America, looking for both financial gain and religious freedom.

■ How the Colonists Stole Christmas

Struggling with biting cold, flu-like infections ("the great sickness"), and lack of food, the pilgrims barely survived their first few months in their new home. Half of them died. Ten of the 17 male heads of families died during the first infection and 14 of the 17 wives died within three months. With survival as a main concern, the first Christmas passed without much comment. By the second year, however, the colonists were no longer simply trying to stay alive. Governor William Bradford informally banned Christmas that year, though it was not until 1659 that the ban was written into law:

> [I]t is therefore ordered by this court and the authority thereof that whosoever shall be found observing any such day as Christmas or the like, either by forbearing of labor, feasting, or any other way, upon any such account as aforesaid, every such person so offending shall pay for every such offence five shilling as a fine to the county.
> –Massachusetts Bay Colony General Court, May 11, 1659

Bradford came from the Massachusetts Bay settlement north of Plymouth, in the area that is now Boston. The settlers in this area were called Puritans. Unlike the Pilgrims, they did not wish to separate completely from the Church of England. They thought they could reform it from within by using themselves as an example of religious purity. Though the Puritans and Pilgrims saw themselves as quite different from each other, in reality they shared a number of beliefs.

Both the Pilgrims and the Puritans believed that all humankind was going to end up in hell, with the exception of a select few people, known as the "elect." Through God's grace, they would be spared. However, there was no way of knowing who was one of the elect. What role a person played in God's plan was predetermined. God decided his or her fate before someone was born. Good behavior would not change a person's fate, but bad behavior often led to serious results. It was also considered a sign that a person was not one of the elect. Given this setting, one can understand why the colonial leaders wanted nothing to do with Christmas. For one thing, they despised its pagan origins–the drinking, dancing, feasting, and general freedom from rules. In the late 1500s, Philip Stubbes, a strict English Protestant, expressed it this way: "More mischief is that time committed than in all the year besides . . . What dicing and carding, what eating and drinking, what banqueting and feasting is then used . . . to the great dishonour of God and the impoverishing of the realm." (Johnston 1918)

The New England settlers also banned Christmas because they associated it with Catholicism, which they rejected. They wanted to get rid of anything connected with the Catholic tradition: incense, candles, vestments, statues, and other objects common to Catholic churches. By trimming away observance of holidays such as Christmas, Lent, Easter, or festivals of the saints, they believed they would get closer to God. Their Sabbath worship took place in "plain style": sitting on hard wooden benches in a simple, unheated church (the Meeting House) for two hours or more of praying, singing psalms (songs praising God) and listening to a sermon. If someone dozed off during a long reading, a person called the "tithing" man came around with his long pole and poked them awake.

NEW ARRIVALS

In early America newcomers had to keep their Christmas celebrations secret so the Puritans would not punish them. Non-Puritans who arrived in the colonies quickly found that the magistrates and clergy would not allow them to observe Christmas as they had in their countries of origin. Some tried celebrating in secret, but the church had ways of finding out about hidden festivities. Friends and neighbors snooped on each other in order to gain favor with the minister and (they hoped) in the eyes of God. Some towns went so far as to appoint official snoops, who each kept track of the private affairs of ten of their neighbors. People who criticized or rebelled against the government were seen as rebelling against God. As the years wore on, the congregations were ruled more and more by their councils of elders, and less and less by equality among town members. For the descendants of the original settlers, Christmas was exotic, alien, and forbidden. For people who could be hauled into court and fined for wearing silk, "coasting" on the ice, or swimming (such activities were considered an immoral waste of time), December 25 had become just an ordinary day.

Christmas might never have reappeared in New England if not for the arrival of new immigrants from Europe during the 17th and 18th centuries. As the population grew in number and differing nationalities, it became harder and harder for the church and government to control the beliefs of individuals. Christmas became more and more accepted, although it did not become an official holiday until 1856. Finally, 27 years after it became law, the law fining people for feasting or observing Christmas was repealed.

For the Dutch, Christmas was always a time to be joyous and to take time off from one's daily tasks. They, along with the German immigrants, turned Christmas into a family-centered holiday. For example, December 14, 1654, the city fathers of New Amsterdam ordered the city corporation to hold no more meetings until three weeks after Christmas. No court messengers were allowed to summon anyone during that period, either. Though the Dutch had settled less than 285 miles from the Puritans, their attitude toward Christmas was obviously very different.

When the British took over New Amsterdam, they brought their own Christmas traditions with them. Their gift-giver was called Father Christmas. Unlike the thin, shy Saint Nicholas of the

▲ Members of a church youth group pose as a living nativity scene in Columbus, Indiana.

Dutch tradition, Father Christmas was seen as a cheerful, outgoing fellow who lifted people's spirits just by appearing. Gradually, the two figures blended together to form the modern day Santa Claus.

CHRISTMAS FOR THE COLONISTS IN JAMESTOWN
Unlike the Pilgrims and Puritans, there were no restrictions forbidding the colonists of Jamestown to celebrate Christmas as they had in England. The main goal of their trip was to make money, not find religious freedom. Their financial backers, the Virginia Company of London, hoped they would find gold and other natural resources to send back to England. Whereas the Massachusetts colonists arrived with women and children, all of the 104 settlers who sailed up the James River in May 1607 were male.

There were a few farmers among them, and a small group of craftsmen. They were also lucky to have with them Captain John Smith (of Pocahontas fame) who might have exaggerated his exploits but who nevertheless had an amazing survival history. He came to Virginia having already been a soldier, having been enslaved, and having been both a pirate and a mutineer. He also loved Christmas, proclaiming early in the expedition, "Wherever an Englishman may be, and in whatever part of the world, he must keep Christmas with feasting and **merriment**!" (BBC–History. "Ten Ages of Christmas") Such feasting would prove difficult in the years 1609 and 1610, years the early colonists would come to call the "starving time." After generations of hardship and perseverance, however, Virginians by the 18th century were getting to be known for their rich bounty and extravagant displays. Following the pagan tradition of hanging up greens during Christmas, the settlers in Virginia used whatever plant materials they could find during the bleak winter days: berries, evergreens, branches of holly or bay, and any flowers not yet drained of color. The rooms were filled with firelight and candlelight in contrast to the darkness outside.

Get a sense of a colonial Christmas.

Since there are no sources that describe the colonists' interior Christmas decorations, historians rely on 18th-century English prints to make an educated guess. In the few illustrations that remain, a large cluster of mistletoe is the most important feature. There are also sprigs of holly, bay, or other greens in vases or other containers, or sometimes pressed against the windowpanes. Christmas trees were not introduced until later; however, the European tradition of the Yule log was part of their celebration. Since no one was required to do unnecessary work as long as the Yule log burned, servants and slaves are reputed to have soaked the Yule log in water before it was lit, hoping that it would stay burning even longer than the 12 days of tradition.

While the holiday meant a time of good food and merriment for all members of the community, the wealthy were able to put more on their tables. Meats such as beef, goose, ham, and turkey were favorites. Other households also served fish and fresh oysters from the nearby ocean. For desserts, the colonists turned to those they had enjoyed in England. As they were brought steaming and sometimes flaming with brandy to the table, the aromas of cinnamon and clove filled the air. There were favorites such as plum pudding, brandied peaches, or mincemeat pie, topped with hard sauce–essentially a cold, brandy-flavored frosting.

▲ As a land whose European forebears were Christian dissidents looking for religious freedom, the United States has a unique relationship with Christmas. The United States has no official state religion, as many countries do, but Christmas is enjoyed throughout the country. Shown here is the National Christmas Tree outside the Capitol Building in Washington, D.C.

"YANKEE" SANTA

In 1863 during the Civil War, President Lincoln asked Thomas Nash to do a special illustration showing Santa visiting the Union troops. Historians report that many soldiers in the Confederate army became discouraged by seeing Santa take the side of the North.

Because refrigeration was unavailable, dishes often contained a mix of sugar, spices, and alcohol since such ingredients act as preservatives. During medieval times both plum pudding and mincemeat pies contained venison (deer meat) or beef. By the mid-1800s, however, usually the only meat ingredient was suet, or beef fat. (Many modern cooks use vegetable fat instead.) In mincemeat pie the filling consists of dried fruit such as raisins, apples, currants, apricots, candied peel, and spices such as cinnamon or nutmeg. Some versions include nuts, brandy, or rum. Fruitcake is another Christmas food that came from England. In colonial Virginia, wines, brandy, rum punches, and other alcoholic beverages were also plentiful during Christmas, and there existed a tradition of landowners doling out liquor to laborers to reduce their will to stray. Unlike the focus of many modern Christmas activities, there was no thought given to what would amuse children. In fact, children were supposed to behave like small adults.

In the 1800s, interest in Christmas exploded in North America in a way it never had before, helped along by writers and artists who captured the imagination of the people through poems, fiction, and illustrations. Washington Irving, the writer best known for stories such as "The Legend of Sleepy Hollow" and "Rip Van Winkle," published *Knickerbocker's History of New York* in 1809. In it the author describes a jolly Saint Nicholas–type character. His Saint Nicholas was not the tall, shy bishop that had commonly appeared in paintings and sculptures, but a good-natured, pipe-smoking character, not unlike the middle-class Dutchmen he saw every day in the city. A year later, an artist created the first American image of Nicholas in honor of the Saint's day. Nicholas was shown stuffing children's treats into stockings hanging from a fireplace. The accompanying poem ends, "Saint Nicholas, my dear good friend! To serve you ever was my end, If you will, now, me something give, I'll serve you ever while I live."

In a time of social **unrest** and high unemployment, Irving's romantic view of Christmas helped revive an interest in the holiday. In 1821 he published a new *History of New York*, in which he added new details about Saint Nicholas such as "riding over the tops of trees in that self same wagon wherein he brings his yearly presents to children . . . the smoke from his pipe spread like a

▲ Dancers perform the Nutcracker ballet. The ballet with music by Russian composer Pyotr Ilyich Tchaikovsky is a very popular Christmastime entertainment.

cloud overhead ... when he had smoked his pipe, he twisted it in his hatband, and laying his finger beside his nose, gave a very significant look; then mounting his wagon he returned over the tree tops and disappeared."

One year later the poem originally titled "A Visit from Saint Nicholas" (now better known as "Twas the Night Before Christmas") appeared. The author, Clement C. Moore, had clearly been influenced by Irving. Other parts of the poem seem to have come from the author's own imagination. Forty years later, a German-American political cartoonist named Thomas Nash created drawings of Santa Claus that solidified the image introduced by Irving and Moore. Every year, Nash did a new drawing of Santa for New York's *Harper's Weekly* magazine. Later, between 1931 and

1964, the artist Haddon Sundblom did a similar thing for the Coca-Cola Company by creating a new illustration of Santa every year. Around this time also began one of the most enduring American Christmas traditions, the lighting of the Christmas tree in Rockefeller Center in New York City. Since 1933 a tree of no less than 65 feet high and 35 feet wide has been decorated, lit, and displayed for the public. Many Americans–New Yorkers and those beyond–consider it a major event in the start of the Christmas season.

ALMOST SNOWLESS IN SEATTLE

People who live in locations that seldom look like the Christmas shown in picture books have found creative ways to create their own images of Christmas. Those who live on a coastline take advantage of the magical effect created when lights are reflected in water at night. For example, in the Northwest, a ship-to-shore celebration has taken place for 58 years. While on the shore, thousands gather around bonfires. On the water, *The Spirit of Seattle*, the official Christmas ship, floats like an illuminated Christmas ornament, shimmering with hundreds of tiny lights and holiday **garlands**. On board, choirs sing carols and holiday greetings. The sound is broadcast to the bonfire sites on the shore, as well as to other boats. The Christmas Ship cruises to more than 45 waterfront communities, followed by other decorated boats that join in the fun.

CHRISTMAS CELEBRATIONS IN CALIFORNIA

In California, Christmas boat parades are part of Christmas in a variety of seaside locations such as Newport Beach, Huntington Harbor, and San Diego. Disneyland's holiday decorations are usually grand, but visitors can take in light displays from one end of California to the other, including Hearst Castle, and the Roaring Camp Railroad, which runs a special Holiday Lights Train from the mountains down into Santa Cruz. In Yosemite Park, the hotel turns the dining room into a 17th-century English manor for three hours of Christmas carols, Renaissance customs, music, and food. Visitors join the squire and his family, the servants, the Lord of Misrule, minstrels, and other characters in welcoming in the season.

■ Hanukkah in the United States

One of the special ways American Jews have come to celebrate Hanukkah is by linking the miracle of the oil to their concern over the environment. In 1992, former vice president Al Gore and scientist Carl Sagan invited the leaders of Jewish organizations as well as rabbis and Jewish senators to a conference about a Jewish response to the environmental crisis. A year later, the Coalition on the Environment and Jewish Life (COEJL) was created. The purpose of the

▲ A young boy lights a menorah.

HANUKKAH IN NEW YORK CITY

New York City is one of the major centers of the world's Jewish population. Even corner delis may stock Hanukkah candles. Bank windows and other commercial displays will feature menorahs, dreidel decorations, and the Magen David, or Star of David, a blue, six-pointed star that has represented the Jewish homeland since at least the 1890s.

organization was to build a uniquely Jewish approach to conservation, preservation, and other ecological concerns.

Included in the holy writings of Judaism such as the Torah and the Talmud are values such as *tikkun olam* (repairing the world) and *tashchit* (do not waste). In addition, many holy writings contain descriptions of nature as an expression of the Divine, such as this famous quote attributed to Rabbi Abraham ben Moses (1186–1237): "In order to serve God, one needs access to the enjoyment of the beauties of nature, such as the contemplation of flower-decorated meadows, majestic mountains, flowing rivers . . . For all these are essential to the spiritual development of even the holiest people." (COEJL) The tradition of the *mitzvah*, or good deed, is also an essential part of Jewish tradition, and has been for thousands of years.

At the heart of the Hanukkah story, a tiny jar of oil is able to light the menorah for eight days. COEJL sees a parallel between this historical event and the way people generate and use energy. Similarly, rededicating themselves to the natural temple that is Earth, their home, can be a way for Jews to honor the rededication of the temple in Jerusalem. COEJL has put together a number of resources in what they have named *Let There Be (Renewable) Light*.

TEXT-DEPENDENT QUESTIONS

1: How do the Inuit explain the phenomenon of the northern lights?

2: What are *boulettes*, and where are they consumed?

3: What is the original title of the poem now commonly known as "Twas the Night Before Christmas"?

 **RESEARCH PROJECTS**

1: Research the biography of one of the artists or writers mentioned in this chapter, including Clement C. Moore, Thomas Nash, or Haddon Sundblom. Write a brief overview of the artist or writer's life, including where they were born, what other works they were noted for, and their cultural influence.

2: Research the Coalition on the Environment and Jewish Life, including its history, membership, mission statement, and noteworthy projects. Write a brief synopsis of the organization.

▲ Department store Christmas window displays are a popular holiday attraction. Here, people line up outside Saks Fifth Avenue in New York City to view the elaborate installations.

Series Glossary

ancestors The direct family members of one who is deceased

aristocrat A member of a high social class, the nobility, or the ruling class

atonement The act of making up for sins so that they may be forgiven

ayatollah A major religious leader, scholar, and teacher in Shii Islam; the religious leader of Iran

colonial era A period of time between the 17th to 19th century when many countries of the Americas and Africa were colonized by Europeans.

colonize To travel to and settle in a foreign land that has already been settled by groups of people. To colonize can mean to take control of the indigenous groups already in the area or to wield power over them in order to control their human and physical resources.

commemorate To honor the memory of a person or event

commercialization The act of reorganizing or reworking something in order to extract profit from it

descendant One who comes from a specific ancestor

Eastern Orthodox Church The group of Christian churches that includes the Greek Orthodox, Russian Orthodox, and several other churches led by patriarchs in Istanbul (Constantinople), Jerusalem, Antioch, and Alexandria.

effigy A representation of someone or something, often used for mockery

equinox Either of the two times during each year when night and day are approximately the same length of time. The spring equinox typically falls around March 21 and the autumnal equinox around September 23.

fast To abstain from eating for a set period of time, or to eat at only prescribed times of the day as directed by religious custom or law.

feast day A day when a religious celebration occurs and an intricate feast is prepared and eaten.

firsthand From the original source; experienced in person

Five Pillars of Islam The five duties Muslims must observe: declaring that there is only one God and Muhammad is his prophet, praying five times a day, giving to charity, fasting during Ramadan, and making a pilgrimage to Mecca

foundation myth A story that describes the foundation of a nation in a way that inspires its people

Gregorian calendar The calendar in use through most of the world

hedonism The belief that pleasure is the sole good in life

Hindu A follower of Hinduism, the dominant religion of India

imam A leader; a scholar of Islam; the head of a mosque

indigenous Originating in or native to a specific region; often refers to living things such as people, animals, and plants

Islam The religious faith of Muslims. Muslims believe that Allah is the only God, and Muhammad was his prophet

Judaism A religion that developed among the ancient Hebrews. Followers of Judaism believe in one God and follow specific laws written in the Torah and the Talmud, and revealed to them by Moses.

Julian calendar Is named after Julius Caesar, a military leader and dictator of ancient Rome, who introduced it in 46 B.C.E. The Julian calendar has 365 days divided into 12 months, and begins on January 1. An extra day, or leap day, is added every four years (February 29) so that the years will average out to 365.242, which is quite close to the actual 365.242199 days of Earth's orbit.

lower realm In the Asian tradition, the place where the souls end up if their actions on Earth were not good

lunar Related to the Moon

martyr A person who willingly undergoes pain or death because of a strong belief or principle

masquerade A party to which people wear masks, and sometimes costumes or disguises

millennium 1,000 years

monarch A king or queen; a ruler who inherits the throne from a parent or other relative

monotheism The belief in the supremacy of one god (and not many) that began with Judaism more than 4,000 years ago and also includes the major religions of Islam and Christianity.

mosque An Islamic house of worship

mourning The expression of sorrow for the loss of a loved one, typically involving

movable feast A religious feast day that occurs on a different day every year

Muhammad The prophet to whom God revealed the Quran, considered the final prophet of Islam

mullah A clergyman who is an expert on the Quran and Islamic religious matters

Muslim A person who follows the Islamic religion

New Testament The books of the Bible that were written after the birth of Christ

New World A term used to describe the Americas from the point of view of the Western Europeans (especially those from France, England, Portugal, and Spain) who colonized and settled what is today North and South America.

offering Donation of food or money given in the name of a deity or God

Old Testament The Christian term for the Hebrew Scriptures of the Bible, written before the birth of Christ

oral tradition Stories told aloud, rather than written, as a way to pass down history

pagan Originally, someone in ancient Europe who lived in the countryside; a person or group that does not believe in one god, but often believes in many gods that are closely connected to nature and the natural world

pageantry Spectacle, elaborate display

parody Imitation of something, exaggerated for comic effect—for example, a parody of science fiction movies.

patria Fatherland; nation; homeland

peasant People who farm land that usually belongs to someone else, such as a landowner

penance The repentance of sins, including confessing, expressing regret for having committed them, and doing something to earn forgiveness

piety A strong belief in and correspondingly fervent practice of religion

pilgrimage A journey undertaken to a specific destination, often for religious purposes

prank A mischievous or humorous trick

pre-Columbian Of or relating to the period before Christopher Columbus arrived in the Americas

procession A group of people moving together in the same direction, especially in a type of celebration

prophecy A prediction about a future event

prophet An individual who acts as the interpreter or conveyer of the will of God and spreads the word to the followers or possible followers of a religion. A prophet can also be a stirring leader or teacher of a religious group. Capitalized it refers to Muhammad.

Protestant A member of a Christian denomination that does not follow the rule of the pope in Rome and is not one of the Eastern Orthodox Churches. Protestant denominations include Anglicans (Episcopalians), Lutherans, Presbyterians, Methodists, Baptists, and many others.

Quran The holy book of Islam

rabbi A Jew who is ordained to lead a Jewish congregation; rabbis are traditionally teachers of Judaism.

reincarnation The belief in some religions that after a person or animal dies, his or her soul will be reborn in another person or animal; it literally means, "to be made flesh again." Many Indian religions such as Hinduism, Sikhism, and Jainism, believe in reincarnation.

repentance To express regret and ask forgiveness for doing something wrong or hurtful.

requiem A Mass for the souls of the dead, especially in the Catholic Church

revel To celebrate in a joyful manner; to take extreme pleasure

ritual A specific action or ceremony typically of religious significance

sacred Connected with God or religious purposes and deemed worthy of veneration and worship

sacrifice Something given up or offered in the name of God, a deity or an ancestor.

shaman A spiritual guide who a community believes has unique powers to tell the future and to heal the sick. Shamans can mediate or cooperate with spirits for a community's advantage. Cultures that practice shamanism are found all over the world still today.

Shia A Muslim sect that believes that Ali, Muhammad's son-in-law, should have succeeded Muhammad as the caliph of Islam; a common sect in Iran but worldwide encompassing only about 15 percent of Muslims

solar calendar A calendar that is based on the time it takes Earth to orbit once around the Sun

solar Related to the Sun

solilunar Relating to both the Sun and Moon

solstice Day of the year when the hours of daylight are longest or shortest. The solstices mark the changing of the seasons–when summer begins in the Northern Hemisphere (about June 22) and winter begins in the Northern Hemisphere (about December 22).

spiritual Of or relating to the human spirit or soul, or to religious belief

Sunni The largest Islamic sect, including about 85 percent of the world's Muslims

supernatural Existing outside the natural world

Talmud The document that encompasses the body of Jewish law and customs

Torah Jewish scriptures, the first five books of the Hebrew scriptures, which serve as the core of Jewish belief

veneration Honoring a god or a saint with specific practices

vigil A period in which a person stays awake to await some event

Vodou A religion rooted in traditional African beliefs that is practiced mostly in Haiti, although it is very popular in the West Indies as well. Outside of Haiti it is called *Vodun*.

Further Resources

■ Books

Major World Religions: Christianity. By Aaron Bowen. Published in 2018 by Mason Crest, Broomall, Pennsylvania. The history of Christianity. Provides information about the beliefs shared by most Christians, details the major sects, and explores festivals and holy days.

Major World Religions: Judaism. By Adam Lewinsky. Published in 2018 by Mason Crest, Broomall, Pennsylvania. Recounts the history of Judaism, providing information about the beliefs shared by most Jews, the three main branches of the faith, and festivals and holy days.

Hebrew Illuminations: A Coloring Journey Through the Jewish Holy Days. By Adam Rhine. Published in 2016 by Amber Lotus Publishing, Portland, Oregon. A coloring book for all ages featuring intricate Judaic motifs, such as Magen Davids, menorahs, and Hebrew calligraphy, for you to bring to vivid life. Each illustration is paired with verses from the Torah, Psalms, and the Prophets that enlighten the reader.

The Origins of Christmas. By Joseph F. Kelly PhD. Published in 2014 by Liturgical Press, Collegeville, Minnesota. The story of the origins of Christmas from pre-Christmas beginnings to Christmas as an integral part of Christian life and Western culture. Brief but full of information.

Your Guide to the Jewish Holidays: From Shofar to Seder. By Cantor Matt Axelrod. Published in 2015 by Rowman & Littlefield Publishers, Lanham, Maryland. Humorous, light-hearted look at the 11 most important Jewish holidays. Explores the historical origins, rituals, and traditional foods associated with each holiday.

The Man Who Invented Christmas: How Charles Dickens's A Christmas Carol Rescued His Career and Revived Our Holiday Spirits. By Les Standiford. Published in 2017 by Broadway Books, New York. The story of how Charles Dickens created his classic Christmas tale.

The Carols of Christmas: A Celebration of the Surprising Stories Behind Your Favorite Holiday Songs. By Andrew Gant. Published in 2016 by Thomas Nelson, Nashville, Tennessee. Smart humorous history of beloved Christmas carols and how they changed over centuries and across countries.

Christmas: A History. By Mark Connelly. Published in 2012 by I.B. Tauris, New York. The story of how modern Christmas came to be from it's pagan and Anglo-German origins to the contemporary notion of Christmas as a reflection of family values.

■ Web Sites

Algonquin Language. http://www.native-languages.org. A comprehensive site about Native American languages, including histories, dictionaries, and current speakers.

Central Moravian Church. http://www.victoriana.com/christmas/putz.htm. Description of the putz tradition and purpose, as well as other Moravian religious traditions.

Colonial Williamsburg. http://www.history.org. Site sponsored by the Colonial Williamsburg Foundation includes information about visiting the attraction in Virginia, as well as links to various articles on colonial life, such as Christmas customs, Captain John Smith, and the African American experience.

Epicurious.com. https://www.epicurious.com/search/hanukkah?content=. Hanukkah recipes ranging from potato latkes to cream cheese Hanukkah stars.

Hanukkah: 8 Days of Action. http://www.coejl.org/resources/hanukkah-8-days-of-action/. Article exploring ways to boost environmental awareness and pro-environment activities during Hanukkah.

The History Channel. http://www.history.com/topics/holidays/hanukkah. A portion of the History Channel's website dedicated to Hanukkah.

Virtual Jamestown. http://www.virtualjamestown.org. For further information about the difficulties confronted by the Jamestown settlement, including interactive activities.

The Master Gardeners. http://www.emmitsburg.net/gardens/articles/adams/2001/yule_log.htm. Site explaining the origins of the Yule log.

National Confectioners Association. https://www.candyusa.com/candy-types/candy-canes/. Details the story of how candy canes came to be a part of every Christmas in the United States.

The Origin of American Christmas Myth and Customs. http://www.arthuriana.co.uk/xmas/swartz/American%20Christmas%20Origins.htm. An extensive article written by professor emeritus of anthropology B. K. Swartz, Jr. of Ball State University (Indiana), on the myths surrounding Christmas and Christmas customs. Includes a timeline showing the earliest known origins of American Christmas customs.

Rebecca Nurse Homestead. http://www.rebeccanurse.org. Site covering the live and customs of colonial New England, dedicated to a Puritan settler named Rebecca Nurse.

Religion and the Founding of the American Republic. http://loc.gov/exhibits/religion. Site dealing with the connection between religion and the various groups of immigrants who came to the United States, including Jews, Quakers, Germans, and others.

Index

Advent calendar, 21-23, 55
Ashkenazi Jews, 42, 43, 44, 51, 73

Bethlehem, 12, 23, 26, 27, 75, 82
Black Friday, 23
Boxing day, 63-64

caroling. *See* Christmas carols
A Christmas Carol (Dickens), 21
Christmas carols, 66, 76, 94, 102
Christmas Mass, 13, 28
Christmastide, 61
Christmas trees, 17, 51, 53, 54, 58-59, 69, 70, 82, 87, 89, 92, 98, 102
Church of the Nativity, 12, 83
crèche, 28, 53, 92

Ded Moroz (Grandfather Frost), 58
Dickens, Charles, 19, 21
dreidels. *See* S'vivon

Epiphany, 11, 27, 62

Father Christmas, 49, 52, 58, 69, 87, 92, 93, 96
frankincense, 28

gelt, 44, 72, 83
"Good King Wenceslas," 63
Grandfather Frost. *See* Ded Moroz

Hanukkah. *See also* S'vivon, 8, 31-45
  customs of, 38-39
  dates to celebrate, 40
  foods symbolism on, 42
  historical importance of, 31-38
  miraculous oil burning, 38
  song of, 37, 45
  spelling variations of, 33
Hasideans, 34-35
Hellenism, 31, 33, 35
Herod I (King), 28

Jesus Christ, 8, 12, 26
Joseph, 26-27, 65, 75

Maccabees, 34, 38, 93
Maccabeus, Judas, 38
magi. *See* three wise men
manger, 28, 53, 61, 70, 83, 89
Mary, 12, 19, 26-27, 65, 75
menorahs, 8, 33, 35, 38, 41, 42, 51, 63, 72, 73, 83, 84, 85, 104
Messiah, 12
Midnight masses, 25, 51, 53, 55, 73
mistletoe, 15, 16, 92, 98
Moore, Clement Clarke, 21, 101
Mummers, 64, 65, 92
myrrh, 28

nativity, 26, 28, 69, 70, 73, 82, 83, 89, 92, 97
La Navidad, 69, 74
Nazareth, 11, 26, 74
Nicholas (Saint), 23-25, 50, 52, 96, 100
"The Night Before Christmas," 21, 25, 101
Noche Buena (Holy Night), 75, 78

Père Noël. *See* Father Christmas
piñatas, 76, 77, 78
posadas, 74, 75, 78
Ptolemy, 32-33

Saint Stephen's Day, 63
Santa Claus, *See also* Ded Moroz; Father Christmas; Nicholas (Saint), 23-25, 58, 73, 82, 87, 88 89, 97, 101
Sephardic Jews, 42, 50
"Silent Night" (Mohr and Gruber), 54
Star of David, 8, 104
S'vivon (dreidels), 8, 42, 43-45, 83, 104

three wise men, 23, 26, 27-28
tinsel, 53-54, 89
"Twas the Night Before Christmas" (Moore), 21, 101
"Twelve Days of Christmas," 21

Virgin Mary. *See* Mary
"A Visit from St. Nicholas," 25
wreaths, 15, 87

Yule logs, 15, 52, 64, 98

Picture Credits

COVER
(Clockwise from top left) iStock/monkeybusinessimages; iStock/pushlama; iStock/Angelafoto; iStock/MargoeEdwards

INTERIOR
7, Shutterstock/Rrajji; 9, iStock/Alex; 10, Shutterstock/ruskpp; 12, iStock/jcarillet; 14, Shutterstock/ Igor_Astakhovi; 15, Shutterstock/Fotosr52; 16 (top), Shutterstock/Billion Photos; 16 (bottom), Shutterstock/Kuttelvaserova Stuchelova; 17, Library of Congress; 20, Shutterstock/lazyllama; 22, Shutterstock/Sven Hansche; 24, Shutterstock/Orest lyzhechka; 26, Shutterstock/Anneka; 27, Shutterstock/Iakov Filimonov; 29, Shutterstock/1000 Words; 30, iStock/DanGonzalez; 32, Musée du Louvre/De Tott Collection, gift before 1805; 33, Shutterstock/Lowe Llaguno; 35, iStock/titoslack; 36, Shutterstock/Valentin Sama-Rojo; 39, iStock/JodiJacobson; 41, Shutterstock/ChameleonsEye; 43, Shutterstock/Ildi Papp; 44, Shutterstock/Sean Locke Photography; 46, iStock/chameleonseye; 47, Shutterstock/Sergei25; 48, iStock/duncan1890; 50, Creative Commons/Matthias Zepper; 52, Shutterstock/Petr Kovalenkov; 53, Shutterstock/Mapics; 54, iStock/rusm; 55, iStock/Wicki58; 58, Shutterstock/E.Kryzhanivskyi; 59, Shutterstock/volkova natalia; 62, Shutterstock/Pres Panayotov; 65, iStock/FrozenShutter; 68, Shutterstock/MindStorm; 70, iStock/holgs; 71, iStock/Devasahayam Chandra Dhas; 74, Shutterstock/MARI TERE; 77 (top), iStock/erlucho; 77 (bottom), iStock/urf; 79, Shutterstock/BestStockFoto; 80, Shutterstock/Daniel Reiner; 84 (top), Shutterstock/dnaveh; 84 (bottom), Shutterstock/ChameleonsEye; 86, Shutterstock/PhotoTrippingAmerica; 88, iStock/pablohart; 93, iStock/windjunkie; 94, iStock/Flory; 97, Shutterstock/Anneka; 99, iStock/Lingbeek; 101, Shutterstock/Pavel L Photo and Video; 103, iStock/tovfla; 105, Shutterstock/DW labs Incorporated